MARTIN LUTHER

The Great Reformer

IMMORTALS OF
PHILOSOPHY AND RELIGION

MARTIN LUTHER
The Great Reformer

BY W. NORMAN PITTENGER, S.T.D.

Franklin Watts, Inc.
575 Lexington Avenue
New York, N.Y. 10022

Also by the author

The Life of Jesus Christ

The Life of Saint Paul

Jacket photo courtesy
New York Public Library Picture Collection
and Collection Goudstikker

First Edition

CONTENTS

PREFACE

I am writing these words only a few hundred yards
from the place where the "great affirmation" was
first proclaimed in the English-speaking world—the
Church of Saint Edward in Cambridge, England.
From the church pulpit (the same one which the
visitor can see today), Hugh Latimer preached a
famous sermon on "justification by grace through
faith," affirming the Christian belief which, according to Reformation theologians, was "the article of a
standing or falling Church." A hundred yards or so
farther on stood the White Horse Tavern, now re-
placed by a building of my own college here in
Cambridge. In one of the tavern rooms Cambridge
theologians once gathered to hear reports about
Martin Luther and his activities in Germany.

From these beginnings the continental Reformation made its initial impact on England, and thence, on the whole English-speaking world. This is why I find a peculiar satisfaction in writing of the life and work of the great German reformer. Whether we are Lutherans, those Christians who look to Luther as their founder; Protestants, who regard Luther's movement as a special heritage; whether we are Roman Catholics, Anglicans, Eastern Orthodox Christians, or non-Christians, we cannot deny the greatness of Luther or the importance of his work. It is interesting that modern Roman Catholic scholars, such as the distinguished German theologian Hans Kung, are recognizing Luther's importance.

Martin Luther is an important figure for us all, whatever our religious allegiance. He is an immortal of history—not only religious history but the history of Germany, Europe, and the whole world. In this book I have tried to show why.

I owe much gratitude to a great many scholars for their help in this work. I have profited by reading books, some very learned and some fairly popular, to assist me in getting the right perspective. The included bibliography is by no means complete. I have selected works that may interest anybody who wishes to read further about Luther and his influence, but I make no pretense of including everything. I have also been helped by historians and theological scholars who are my friends here in Cambridge and elsewhere. To list them would be to inflict upon the reader an intolerably long collection of names, so I thank them in this general way.

I hope that my readers will come away with a better understanding of the man who was one of the chief formative influences of the culture which all of us share today.

W. NORMAN PITTENGER

King's College
Cambridge, England

MARTIN LUTHER

The Great Reformer

CHAPTER I

At the Diet of Worms

The place was the German city of Worms. The occasion was a meeting of the "diet" (a court session), called by Charles V of Spain, who had lately become emperor of the so-called Holy Roman Empire. This slowly fading domain, which in principle included the vast area of central Europe, had at its head the heir of many generations of European Catholic sovereigns. The emperor did not inherit his position, however. He was chosen by ruling princes of the realm, and Charles had been elected following the death of his grandfather, Maximilian.

The purpose of the diet was to consider serious problems facing the Empire, specifically the rising rebellion against the authority of the established Catholic Church. The man believed to be responsible for the rebellion was Dr. Martin Luther, a young German theologian who taught at the University of Wittenberg. Luther had dared to publish charges against the authorities of the Church, alleging abuses and corruption. He had posted a series of short statements, called "theses," on the church door at Wittenberg, and he had engaged in debates with official representatives of the Church. In these debates he seemed to be the spokesman for a discontent which hitherto had been more or less hidden.

Luther had been "invited" to appear at the diet, although the invitation was much more like a summons. He was to answer charges which were based on some twenty-five books and pamphlets that he had written. The young theologian was not anxious to appear, for he was sure that his life would be in danger. However, he had received "safe-conduct" from the emperor, which was supposed to guarantee his safety.

The date of the meeting was April 16, 1521, and the sessions continued for several days. The great moment—one of the critical moments in world his-

tory—came in the late afternoon and early evening
of April 18.

On the preceding day, Luther had been shown
copies of his books. He had acknowledged them as
his, but when he was asked to retract what he had
written, he had reserved his answer, saying that he
needed time to determine just what his response
would be. He was given the night to make up his
mind, and throughout that night and for most of the
next day he is reported to have worked on his answer.

At four o'clock on the afternoon of April 18, Luther was taken to a large hall where a great crowd
had gathered. He had to wait outside the hall until
six o'clock, by which time it had become rather dark
and candles had been lighted. Luther was ordered to
give his answer, responding to the charges and saying whether he would recant, or take back, what he
had written.

As part of his answer, Luther analyzed his books,
speaking first of the parts which were ordinary
Christian devotional writing, and then of the sec-
tions in which he had made criticisms of the Church,
especially of the papacy and its role. He said that he
could not take back what he had written about the
papacy. If he did so, more evil might arise in the
Church; the corruption might grow. Concerning
those parts of his books where he had directly at-

5

tacked individuals, Luther admitted that perhaps he had spoken more violently than he should have.

Now came the crucial question, asked by Dr. Johann Eck, who represented the official Church hierarchy. "I ask you, Martin, that you respond candidly and without equivocation. Do you or do you not repudiate your books and the errors which they contain?" Eck was impatient with Luther's careful distinctions between the various parts of his writings. The representative wanted a wholesale recantation —nothing other, nothing less.

Then came Luther's reply—one of history's famous utterances.

"Since Your Majesty [the Holy Roman Emperor, presiding at the meeting] and your lordships [the other rulers and high officials present] desire to have from me a simple answer, I will answer 'without horns and without teeth.' Unless I am convinced by Scripture and by plain reason—for I do not accept the authority of popes and councils, since they contradict one another and since they have often erred —I am bound by my conscience, I am held captive by the Word of God as this is found in the words of Scripture which I have quoted. I cannot recant and I will not recant anything, because it is entirely wrong to go against conscience, and because it is never safe to go against it. God help me! Amen!"

Those are the recorded words found in the early

printed versions of Luther's speech. But in those same versions some further words are found. There is no reason to doubt that Luther also said them. These are the most famous words attributed to him: "Here I stand. I cannot do otherwise!"

A celebrated drawing of Luther at the Diet of Worms quotes him this way: *Hier stehe ich. Ich kann nicht anders. Gott helfe mir. Amen.* ("I stand here. I can do nothing beyond what I have done. God help me. Amen.")

That scene in April, 1521, was a turning point in the history of Europe, indeed of the world. And it helps us to understand why Martin Luther is so important a person in the world's history.

First, that scene was the beginning of the division of western Christianity into the two groups which we call Catholic and Protestant. What Luther said and did, symbolized by this one dramatic scene at Worms, was the decisive factor in bringing about this division.

Second, Luther's assertion at the Diet of Worms that it was his conscience which was at stake is crucial in showing that a man must be prepared to risk literally everything in order to be true to his conscience. Of course, people had respected and obeyed their consciences long before Luther lived. But Luther's flat statement, in such plain and unmistakable words, might be called the point in time when this truth about conscience was publicly stated in terms that nobody could escape.

Third, what Luther said about being "held captive by the Word of God as this is found in Scripture" is a clear profession of the importance of the Bible in all Christian thinking and teaching. The Bible has always been absolutely essential to all Christians. Yet Luther's words made its importance explicit. He challenged all Christian religious institutions. He insisted on loyalty to the Scriptures. Luther spoke for all those who in later ages have called themselves Protestant. And even now, more than four hundred and fifty years later, he is making his influence felt in the Roman Catholic Church itself. At the Vatican Council held a few years ago, many distinguished Catholic scholars accepted Luther's point—it is the Bible, not traditional Church teaching or anything else, which must be the final court of appeal for Christians in matters of faith.

Fourth, Luther's appearance at the Diet of Worms marks the beginning of self-conscious German nationalism and, therefore, of nationalism elsewhere in Europe and the New World. For Luther won the support of many fellow Germans. He became a spokesman for the spirit of the German people.

Finally, because the Lutheran cause received much help from the rising mercantile classes in Germany and elsewhere, the Diet of Worms represents, symbolically, the appearance of a new type of social pattern in western European history. Doubtless, Luther did not actually intend this, for in many ways he belonged to the Middle Ages and its pattern of society. But his movement profoundly altered social structures, ending the feudal age and bringing about a world where the middle classes have had dominance.

These five points illustrate the historical importance of Martin Luther. And one more may be added. Among all the great characters in history, Luther is one of the most fascinating and colorful. His career was marked by a series of dramatic crises. His own personal character was extraordinary, for he was a religious genius and a great scholar but also a very warm and vital personality. He translated the Bible into German and in doing so, practically "created" the German language. It was his use of his native tongue, his kind of Germanic idiom or phraseology, and his vivid and compelling literary style which, for the first time, brought the German language to its classical perfection. Not that he wrote in a stiff and formal way; on the contrary, his German was very free, very vernacular, and easily understandable. What he did do, however, was to permit the German language to stand on its own, somewhat in the same way that early English writers, after Chaucer, were able to write English freely and simply because that great poet had given his language a character entirely its own.

The German of Luther's Bible, of his hundreds of essays on books of the Bible, of his miscellaneous articles, and, above all, of his letters and his *Table Talk*—what his friends remembered and wrote down from his conversations—demonstrates a well-known saying: *The style is the man*. Luther's German— vivid, clear, strong, colorful, and sometimes romantic—is exactly like the man who wrote and spoke that German.

The story of Luther's life involves his vigor in defense of what he believed to be true. It also involves his tenderness, shown, for example, in letters to his son. He had a great capacity for righteous indignation when he believed that some evil was being done and he felt outraged by that evil. There were times when he spoke and wrote in an earthy manner. He could be almost vulgar in his plain speaking, when he thought that such plain speaking was necessary.

Luther himself was just like his writings and speeches. He had absolute integrity. Nobody ever had to wonder if what they heard or read represented Luther's deepest personality, or was just a surface pretense. The man rang true all the way through. Even his opponents and his worst enemies were obliged to acknowledge his integrity.

It is this absolute integrity which explains, perhaps more than anything else, why Martin Luther has been called the greatest German who ever lived and why he has been so much the idol of his own people. Even those who do not share his religious beliefs, and would never think of themselves as his followers (or Lutherans), still acknowledge him as a great German leader.

In fact, many years ago a distinguished German scholar gave a lecture on the importance of using some outstanding personality as an example, or model. Such an example, he said, would provide a focus for one's loyalties. Instead of naming a leader from the contemporary world, the lecturer suggested Martin Luther—a man who had lived over four hundred years before, whose problems were entirely different from those of the speaker and his audience, whose point of view in so many ways must certainly be called outdated. But it was Luther, said the lecturer, who could be such a model. Why? Because Luther was a man who was absolutely trustworthy, with whom everybody knew exactly where he stood, and whose personal character was that of a righteous, convinced, brave defender of the truth as he saw it.

There have, of course, been many other historical personalities of whom the same could be said—men like Socrates in the ancient world, or Edmund Burke and Oliver Cromwell in Great Britain. There are many in the United States—George Washington, Thomas Jefferson, and Abraham Lincoln. Luther has served in much the same way for many generations of Germans. He has become a symbol of the brave man, standing firmly for what he believes, and at the same time showing those very human characteristics which are delightful to find in someone who has become famous.

Although there is a great deal to know about Martin Luther, the focus of it all is found in that scene at Worms. There stood one rather young man, certainly not tired and worn with the ways of the world. He faced a council composed of princes and prelates, in all their dignity and with all their sense of self-importance. Presiding over the council was the Holy Roman Emperor, a severe and autocratic man of Spanish background. It seemed that the young Luther had not a chance in the world. He would be condemned, imprisoned, perhaps even killed. His teaching, the positions he defended, would be suppressed, and it would all be over in a few days. But on the contrary, it was the young man who really won the victory, whose challenge was not put down, whose voice was not silenced, and whose influence grew.

That picture will long live as a vivid portrayal of the way in which one person—certain of his stand and ready to die for his beliefs—can sway the world and change the face of things. Here is greatness embodied in a man.

CHAPTER
II

Early Years

Martin Luther was born at Eisleben, a copper-mining center in the German county of Mansfeld, on November 10, 1483. His father was Hans Luther, a miner. His mother, Margarete, belonged to a family called Ziegler which had come from the not-distant Eisenach.

It has sometimes been said that Luther's family was of the lowest and most depressed social class, but this was not the case. They were peasants, but they were not utterly impoverished. Indeed, Hans Luther's parents had been small landowners, even

13

though they had possessed little wealth and had been obliged to live economically. Much the same was true of Margarete's family.

If Luther's father had not been one of several children, he might well have inherited the farm which his family owned. But at that time it was customary for the youngest son of a peasant family to receive all the assets, and Hans was not the youngest son. German law made impossible any division of such a farm and its revenues. Therefore, Hans had to go to work in order to support himself. Copper mining was just beginning in the area where he had spent his youth, so this was the obvious work for him to undertake.

After his marriage to Margarete, Hans moved to the town of Eisleben—about a hundred miles away from his childhood home—and there he continued his work in copper mining.

When the Luthers' first child was born, he was named Martin because he was baptized on Saint Martin's Day, which is November 11 in the calendar of the Catholic Church. In religious circles, it was considered auspicious to name a child after the saint whose anniversary fell on the day of the baby's baptism. The ceremony took place in the Church of Saint Peter in Eisleben.

The Luther family may have lived in Eisleben for some time before Martin's birth, but the following year, in the late spring or summer of 1584, they moved to the town of Mansfeld, also a mining center. Once again, Hans worked in the mines, and the family, which soon included several other children, seems to have been happy there.

The area around Mansfeld is very beautiful. The Hartz Mountains are nearby. They are not high peaks like the Alps but are more like the rolling hills of the Appalachian Mountains in the United States. There are also meadows and woods, and, on a cliff overlooking the town itself, stands the ancient and beautiful castle of the counts of Mansfeld, who were the feudal lords of the area.

The beautiful countryside in which the young Luther grew up probably had much to do with his strong love of nature and his sense of belonging to the land. Although his family had advanced from peasant status and were now members of what might be called the lower middle class, like so many Germans who live in rural districts they had a tremendous devotion to the physical setting of their homeland. Germany is a beautiful country, and Luther was typical of his countrymen in loving its natural splendor and varied landscape. Two of the most delightful characteristics of Luther's later writings and speeches are his ability to use plain and homely country illustrations and his down-to-earth references to the simple country life of the German peasantry and small landowners. Martin Luther used to pride himself on his peasant background. His recollections of family talk and manner of living, as well as his knowledge of the hardships which peasants endured, enabled him to speak with remarkable directness to the ordinary German people of his time.

Some of Luther's remarks in later years have given the impression that he had a very difficult childhood. He told of being caned by his mother for some childish fault and of being whipped by his father. After the whipping, he said that he had run away for a while, because he was so upset by his punishment. But it would be wrong to assume that he knew no real family affection. Instead, it should be remembered that in those days the old adage about "sparing the rod and spoiling the child" was taken very seriously. As a writer on Luther once said, people were not "so tender" nor was there "so much permissiveness" in those days.

Yet it seems true that the idea of parental authority, so strong in the Teutonic personality, was dominant in the Luther home. On one occasion, Luther spoke about how one "trembled at each word of his father and mother." Obviously Hans and Margarete were hard workers, struggling to maintain their recently acquired position. Doubtless they were sometimes impatient when their children were unruly and willful and not always appreciative of the effort it had taken to secure for them a reasonable measure of economic security and physical comfort.

On the other hand, Luther's references indicate that his father was often a very affectionate and jolly parent, who played with his children and did what he could to amuse them. Indeed, the affection between Hans and his son was very great, so much so that when Martin later decided not to go into the legal profession, as Hans wished, the boy was greatly grieved because he knew that he had disappointed his father.

As for his mother, even when Luther told of the caning she had given him, he added that she had done it because "she meant well." Margarete Luther was an uneducated woman, and like so many at that time, she shared superstitions and folktales about the way life must be lived in fear of God and the devil. The devil was no fancy bit of imagination in those days, but a very real and terrible figure. In fact, Margarete once believed that a woman who lived near their home was a witch who had cursed the Luther family. This sort of notion was fairly typical of people of her background and lack of education.

On the other hand, she must have been a good mother in many ways. She brought up her children well, taught them to be courteous as well as dutiful, and tried to help them understand that they must never think "more highly of themselves than they ought to think." Martin remembered a little ditty that she once taught them:

> If folk don't like you and me,
> The fault with *us* is likely to be.

Margarete was musical and she loved to sing to her children. It is probably from her that Martin first learned to appreciate music. In any event, as he grew older, Martin himself became a fine singer, and he is directly responsible for the splendid musical tradition which is so much a part of the Lutheran religious movement. It may have also been his mother's influence which gave Luther his gift for simple direct verse. The songs which she sang were straightforward, homespun, and readily understandable. So Luther's own hymns—the best known being "Cradle Song" ("Away in a Manger") and *"Ein Feste Burg"* ("A Mighty Fortress Is Our God")—are simple, direct, and forceful.

Martin Luther himself acknowledged, in his *Table Talk*, the tremendous importance of the home and the absolute necessity of strong family life in the development of character. His later treatment of his own children, his own home, and family life after his marriage to "my Katie" combined something of the severity which he had known with the affection and understanding which he also must have known. Experts in "Luther-research," or the study of Luther's life, no longer accept the idea that the great reformer's early years were miserably unhappy. They recognize that his incidental remarks, such as anyone might make about parents or childhood, cannot be taken as the whole truth.

We know a little of Martin's homelife, but what of his school life? Once again we must recognize the differences in teaching methods and ways of maintaining discipline between the schools of the fifteenth century and those of today. At that time, order was maintained largely through the use of punishment, often physical punishment. Furthermore, the pupil was taught to feel inferior to his teachers, and he was supposed to look up to them as great masters. If some humiliation was involved, that was taken for granted. A student was obliged to learn by "rote" (memorization), and was punished for failure of memory or inability to give exact answers. Luther said that his own school days had been a combination of "purgatory and hell." Again, he was undoubtedly exaggerating a little. Yet the fact that he had been hurt by such bitter experiences led him later to take a strong stand for reforms in teaching methods and administering punishment. As he once put it, the apple and the rod must go together.

Until the age of fourteen, Martin attended the so-called Latin school in the town of Mansfeld. He was a tiny child, and it is said that he was carried to his classes on the backs or the shoulders of older boys. In the Latin schools of the day, the instruction was exactly prescribed. Martin would have been taught

Latin—the *lingua franca,* or common tongue, of the educated world. The services of the Church were conducted in Latin, and the Bible was read in that language, for there were no translations available. Every man who had any hope of achieving a position of importance in the world had to learn Latin, unless he was to be a professional soldier or could achieve a place of respect in a nonintellectual way. The language of the courts was Latin, and since Hans had decided that his son should be a lawyer, it was necessary for the boy to master that tongue.

During those early years, while Martin was learning Latin and receiving some instruction in music, literature, and rhetoric—how to write and express oneself in speech—the young boy was also assisting his family at home. By this time Hans owned a number of foundries where copper was smelted. Yet family life was simple and there were no home luxuries. Margarete regularly went into the nearby forest to get wood for heating the house and cooking. In many ways, it was a hard life for the boy, but he does not seem to have begrudged assisting his parents around the house, or helping in the care of the younger children. However, work at home did not interest him as much as what he was learning at school. He was eager to learn. Much later, his friend Melanchthon would remark that from early years Martin had thirsted for knowledge and had continued to thirst for it throughout his life.

At that time, children matured much more quickly than they are permitted to do today. Boys would enter the great universities—for instance, Oxford or Cambridge in England—at age fourteen or even earlier. They were expected to be intelligent, to know how to look after themselves, and to assume responsibilities beyond their years. On the other hand, they were not left alone. There was always a master to check on them, and they were subjected to a rigorous discipline unlike anything known today. They lived simply, sleeping several to a room on pallets of straw, eating a meager meal in the morning and one good meal later on in the day.

Hans had definite plans for his son, and he wanted him to advance in the world. He did not see his oldest boy as a copper miner, but rather as one who would put to good use the intelligence which he showed at school. So when Martin was fourteen, Hans sent him to Magdeburg to continue his studies. Although Martin's stay in Magdeburg lasted only one year, scholars have concluded that while in the city the young student must first have encountered the Brethren of the Common Life, whose simplicity and piety seem to have influenced him deeply.

At Magdeburg, the Brethren of the Common Life had a monastery which was often visited by students in the town. Using their own simple translations of parts of the text, the brethren taught the young men to study the Scriptures. This was a fellowship which

21

stressed the stark simplicity of the Christian life, and this was a community where sympathy and love were shown to all. The Brethren of the Common Life, very German in their outlook and attitude, had something of the quality of the early Franciscans in Italy. They were not wanderers, but lived together in the "common life" which their name implied. They tried to follow the pattern of humility, tranquillity, trusting faith, and common sharing of the good things of the world, which is associated with Saint Francis of Assisi.

One day in Magdeburg, Martin saw Prince Wilhelm of Anhalt begging through the town. The young boy was enormously impressed. Magdeburg was famous for its many churches and for the great religious festivals which took place there. But here was a man of noble family, thin from fasting and religious austerity, going about the streets of the city. Unlike the well-dressed and fat church officials, this was a person who seemed to have grasped something of the spirit of the Christian life as it was understood by those who would be literal followers of Jesus Christ. "When I saw him," said Luther at a later time, "I could not avoid deep emotion and, like everyone, I was ashamed of the secular life." Here, perhaps, was the first moment when the young man felt that he might have a call to become a monk. Wilhelm of Anhalt was a supporter of the Franciscan

fraternity, vowed to poverty and to securing his livelihood by begging alms.

Such incidents as this doubtless had a part in
creating in Luther a feeling that the only way for
him to secure "salvation" would be to embrace a
non-secular life. Within a few years, he would dis-
avow this division between the "religious" and the
"secular"; but during his early years the distinction
seems to have been very plain to him. Yet, for the
moment he did not act on it.

After his year at Magdeburg, Martin went to
Eisenach, his mother's family home. There he continued his education, from 1498 to 1501, at what
seems to have been an excellent school. He later spoke
with special warmth of one of his teachers. This
man, whose name was Trebonius, was a devoted
master who showed tremendous respect for learning.
Luther said that when Trebonius came into the room
where his students were assembled, he always made a
gesture with his academic cap to indicate that he revered these young boys, scholars who one day would
become great masters and leaders of the people, and
whom it was now his privilege to teach.

The point of Martin's study at Eisenach was to prepare him for entrance into the university. This was
not easy, for it was necessary to show academic competence and to meet the requirements with distinction. Although he worked hard, Martin was a typi-

cal student at Eisenach. Like other young scholars, he would wander through the streets, singing for anyone who would listen and accepting gifts to help meet the cost of his education. Martin had an excellent voice, and he had profited by the music instruction which he had already received.

Thanks to this gift for music, the young Luther found a "home away from home" at Eisenach. His singing attracted the attention of the Cotta family. The father was a businessman of considerable means. His wife, Ursula, was a woman of high standards, generosity, good character, and gentle manners. Luther was made a member of the Cotta household, acting as a tutor for the young children. He was happy in their home, where he learned much about good manners, social refinement, and the sort of behavior which would commend a young student to others. Luther had come from a family which was fairly rough, even if not deprived.

Frau Cotta gave the young tutor some knowledge of a cultured and educated family life. And he also learned something else. The devotion of this wife to her husband later influenced Luther's own teaching about Christian marriage: "There is no greater gift in the world than the gift of her love which a wife can make to her husband." Family affection, the sharing of life between husband and wife, and the wifely devotion to husband came to mean much to Martin Luther. For him, this *was* Christian mar-

24

riage. Regrettably, Luther did not say more about
the love of husband for wife, although he insisted
on its necessity. This omission was largely a reflection of the age in which he lived, rather than any
lapse of his own feeling.

In the year 1501, at the age of eighteen, Martin
Luther entered the famous University of Erfurt.
Here were some two thousand students, drawn from
many parts of Germany. They were typical students,
intellectually curious but also likely to be somewhat
dissipated. Not Luther, however. Intellectual curiosity, yes; but a dissipated life, no. In fact, the
friends he made among his fellow students called
themselves "the poets." They spent their spare time
writing essays and papers which were criticized and
discussed at their frequent meetings.

After one year, Luther was granted the degree of
Bachelor of Arts. Although he did not make a particularly notable record during that first year—he
ranked thirtieth in his group of less than sixty—he
was a hard-working and devoted student. His main
concern was philosophy, and his recreational activities included not only meetings with the other
"poets" but also learning to play the lute. He became interested in the lute because of an accident.
Returning to his home from the university, he fell
and suffered a wound in his leg. Since he was wear-
ing the "academic sword"—part of the attire of the
German students of the time—he cut his leg very

badly. During his convalescence, young Luther had little to do, so he passed the time by teaching himself to play the lute. Ever afterward, lute playing was one of the great delights of his leisure moments. His love of music, his robust voice, and his ability to play an instrument gave him a nickname among his fellow students—"the Musician."

But young Luther was also called by another nickname. Because of his keen interest in his major subject, his friends also called him "the Philosopher."

The accepted philosophical outlook during much of the Middle Ages had been set forth in the great *Summae* of Saint Thomas Aquinas, who, in the thirteenth century, had worked out a reconciliation between Christian faith and the philosophy of the newly recovered writings of the Greek thinker Aristotle. In that synthesis, a primary consideration was that human reason, while not able to comprehend the whole range of things, is a valuable and necessary instrument which men can use in their effort to understand the world. Furthermore, human reason could be a "handmaid to faith," by providing the initial steps to explain the existence of the world through the existence of God. "Faith does not overthrow reason; it perfects it." This was the great maxim of the Thomist type of thought.

But in the thinking of an English theologian called William of Ockham, the competence of human reason in matters of faith was severely questioned. Not that the Ockhamists were against reason; indeed, they were very keen logicians and were prepared to use human reason very extensively, but not as a way to prove anything about Christian faith. Faith was human acceptance of what was divinely revealed. Only by God's own self-disclosure could anybody come to genuine knowledge of Him.

At the same time, the Ockhamists put great stress on human will in matters of faith and conduct. Unlike Saint Thomas, who believed that man's reason was his distinctive characteristic, these men felt that man's will was central. Hence, they are often called "voluntarists," or believers in will, as opposed to "rationalists," or believers in reason. Neither did they agree with the older tradition which held that there is a very close relationship between human understanding and the actual facts of the world, so close that one's theory of knowledge could be called "realist"—that is, we do know the reality of *what is*. The position of the Ockhamists was "nominalistic," meaning that human knowledge and naming of things was a matter of human convenience and classification. They were not necessarily what actually exists.

At Erfurt, Luther was taught Ockhamist voluntarism and nominalism. He was taught that human reason is not always to be trusted, while the authority of revelation is absolutely trustworthy. In his later life, even when he engaged in violent and some-

27

times unfair attacks on "scholastic philosophy"—
the name given to all types of philosophy then
taught in the schools—Luther always retained his
conviction that reason is a weak tool, however useful,
and that God's revelation of Himself is the basic
truth. When Luther later attacked the established
theology of the Catholic Church in Europe, he was
not criticizing the faith, but human reason as he understood it to be. He did not reject divine authority;
he rejected placing that authority in the Church itself rather than in God and in God alone. To the end
of his days, Martin Luther was both a voluntarist
and, in his insistence on the incompetence of reason
(apart from faith) to lend meaning to God, a nomi-
nalist.

On January 7, 1505, at the age of twenty-one,
Luther graduated from Erfurt with the degree of
Master of Arts. He had now taken the first steps toward the legal profession which his father intended
for him.

His family was very proud of his achievement; his
father was so proud that he presented Luther with a
very expensive copy of the famous *Corpus Juris*, or
Compendium of Law. Also, since his son had now
achieved academic distinction, the father called him
Ihr, the courteous second person form, instead of the
intimate family term *Du*, or "Thou." Although today this may seem a matter of little importance, at
that time it was an indication of the reverence which

the noneducated felt for the educated and of the affectionate respect of a proud parent toward a child. And Luther returned his father's affection. Even though he would disappoint him in his choice of profession, Luther listened to his father, talked with him on most intimate terms, and obeyed his desires as far as possible without violating his own deep convictions and vows.

Now Hans wanted his son to go on with his studies, and perfect his legal knowledge. Perhaps he would marry a girl of good family, even of wealth. What a splendid prospect that presented!

Certainly, young Martin Luther seemed a fine prospective husband. He was on the short side, and although he later became rather stocky, during his youth he was husky but not stout. He had a strong and healthy body, doubtless the result of his physical labor as a child, and there was nothing of the scholar's pallor about him. He had a rich head of hair, a broad face, and compelling eyes. If not a strikingly handsome young man, he was certainly good-looking. In his own phrase, he was a "peasant" in type, meaning that he looked like a country youth.

Martin's appearance, his musical gifts, his intellectual curiosity, and his sense of humor, which was reported to be keen, helped to make him popular with his fellow students, and he was liked by most people. The iron quality in his character had not yet shown itself.

CHAPTER III

The Late
Middle Ages

The famous poet John Donne, who lived in the late sixteenth and early seventeenth centuries, spoke of the way in which every human being belongs very intimately to the rest of the human race: "No man," he wrote, "is an island entire of itself." Each of us "is a piece of the continent." And so it can be said that we cannot hope to understand ourselves, nor can we know about other people, until we know how we and they fit into the age in which we live.

This is certainly true in trying to understand a man like Martin Luther. He lived in the sixteenth century, and the Church and world of his time profoundly influenced his thoughts and actions.

In the late Middle Ages, the Church was so much a part of human existence, its teaching and activities were so important, that everybody was deeply affected by them. Those years have been called "the age of faith." Even if some people were not personally concerned with what the Church said or did, they were still part of a social structure in which the Church was entirely inescapable. Actually, everybody was taken to be a member of the Church, except for the Jews and the people who were considered "heretics"—those who placed themselves outside the Church by their own choice. But even Jews and heretics did not escape the influence of the Church, so involved was it with every aspect of daily life.

This is a difficult thing for the mid-twentieth-century reader to understand. In the United States, for instance, there is complete separation of the religious, political, economic, and social life. A person may or may not belong to a church. The choice is his. In the late Middle Ages, however—and for centuries before and after—this separation did not exist. The Christian religion and society in general were interrelated. To be a German in the years 1483 to 1546—Luther's lifetime—was also to be a member of the only religious institution which existed, the Catholic Church.

Since everyone but Jews and heretics was considered a Christian, the Church's teachings on personal behavior or social relationships were also the accepted pattern for almost everybody. A person might not always do what he was supposed to do, but he certainly knew what was expected of him. The teachings of the Church were perfectly clear. As a result, civil authorities were always prepared to enforce ecclesiastical teaching. Much that would now be called personal behavior had social implications at that time. In other words, a good deal of "sin" was also understood to be "crime." Although sin concerns a violation of God's will and crime relates to offenses against public order, in Luther's time the two concepts were almost identical.

The Catholic Church was a great monolithic structure. Headed by the pope in Rome, with his *curia*, or court, it had local representatives, the bishops, in each diocese of civilized Europe. Under each bishop, who acted for the pope, were the local clergy, who acted under the orders of the local bishop. Because there were so many small city-states, so many duchies and kingdoms and principalities—each with its own local rulers—the Church was the one all-inclusive institution. Not an inch of the European world was left outside the Church. The whole area was divided into parishes, headed by local priests; the

33

parishes were combined into dioceses, headed by local bishops; and the entire Christian world was the sphere of the Church itself, headed by the pope.

Besides the great numbers of clergy in the parishes, there were dozens of religious orders, or communities of monks or nuns. These orders were communally organized, with houses and chapels. Almost every town in Europe had at least one, perhaps many, and hundreds of thousands of men and women belonged to the orders. Monks and nuns lived under "rule," vowed to observe the so-called "evangelical" command. They could have no personal belongings; they had to live in chastity; and they were obliged to obey their superiors—the priors or abbots of the particular group to which they belonged.

Although no individual in a religious order could own property, the orders themselves were among the biggest property holders of the time. The monastic houses often possessed vast holdings of land and sometimes were extremely rich. So it was with the Church itself. Cathedrals and parish churches, houses of residence for the clergy, and much else were owned by the Church. It was the richest, most powerful establishment on the European scene.

This vast accumulation of worldly possessions was not in the best interests of the Church. Today even Roman Catholic historians agree about this. However, it would be wrong to say that the Church of that time was "wholly corrupt." There were many good, pious, honorable men in the high posts of the Church, as well as among the local clergy, and a large proportion of the "religious" were men and women of sanctity, devotion, and exemplary moral life. Yet it was also true that far too many were grasping, selfish, and anxious to promote their own well-being. This is demonstrated by the simple fact that soon after Luther began his reform, the Catholic Church examined its position and inaugurated the Counter-Reformation, intended to purify the institution and rid it of the all too prevalent corruption.

Nevertheless, the age in which Luther lived was very religious. Every moment of daily existence had religious overtones. Nobody could be entirely secular, for religious devotion and religious practices were found in the home, the shop, the school, the marketplace, and everywhere else.

Hans Luther is a good example of the religious feeling of the time. He believed that his success in copper mining was due not merely to his own efforts and industry but to the fact that Saint Anne, the patron saint of miners, had aided him. God, the Virgin Mary, and the lesser saints were present everywhere. Their help could be invoked by prayer and by promise to contribute to the support of the Church. No area of daily life was without this religious presence or could exist apart from this supernatural control.

35

Often this sense that the "other world" was continually penetrating "this world" led simple people to become superstitious. Besides a belief in witchcraft, sorcery, and the like, there was also the superstition that one could "buy off" the divine powers by a specific act. For instance, divine favor could be secured by promising to make a pilgrimage to some important shrine, or by giving a sum of money to a religious house, or by pledging a son or daughter to the service of the Church. However, along with these superstitions existed a genuine piety. Hans Luther may have been superstitious, but he was also very devout. He prayed regularly with his children. He believed profoundly in God and he wanted to do God's will—although at the same time he had a streak of practical common sense. This is illustrated by one occasion when he was seriously ill. His priest told him that if he gave his money to the Church he could make his peace with God and perhaps be restored to health. The old man replied that God did not need his money so much as his children did; he would give his money to them.

Interestingly enough, in his later teaching Martin, too, recognized the importance of man's ordinary life. He insisted that men had responsibility in the affairs of daily life, and that God himself willed that this should be the case.

People at that time believed strongly in a division between the holy and the ordinary affairs of life. It was a "higher" and a "better" thing to concentrate on the religious rather than on the day-by-day affairs of the world. The best way to be assured of eternal happiness was to enter a religious order or to give oneself directly to the service of God in the Church. One way of life was the way of perfection, found most readily in absolute poverty, chastity, and obedience. The other was the way of compromise, in which the requirements were less exacting and were adapted to the normal life of the ordinary man. If a man denied himself the possibilities of worldly success, he was more certain of finding heavenly security. This was the better way of life, and many were attracted to it, since the fear of eternal damnation, including terrible punishment for failure, was very real. On the other hand, a man could live as good a life as possible under the temptations of the world by doing his job, maintaining his family, and, of course, supporting the Church and the civil government. Then he could hope that God would mercifully pardon all the compromises that he had to make and would grant him eternal happiness after death.

This awareness of a double standard in the Middle Ages helps us to understand Martin Luther's early struggles with his conscience and his fervent desire to find assurance of salvation. In his own words, he wanted "to find a gracious God" who would grant him eternal happiness and a sense of inner peace and security. Although this desire may be difficult for the modern reader, no matter what his religion, to understand, it was very real for Martin Luther and for all those who lived at that time in the Christian culture of Europe.

Yet, people in the Middle Ages were involved not only in the religious side of life. They had social and political concerns as well. And again, those concerns were very different from those with which modern man is most familiar.

The world today is separated into nations, such as the United States, Canada, Italy, or France. In the late Middle Ages, nations as such did not exist, except in the British Isles. Because England is part of an island and fairly small in area, the several kingdoms within it had been able to join together under the centralized authority of a single ruler. The same was true in Scotland, although local loyalties there were still very strong. But on the continent, there was no such thing as the nation of Germany, Italy, or France. Those names might have described a certain land area and the sharing of cultural patterns, but they did not describe a united country, under a central governmental authority.

There were small states all over Europe, some of them consisting of only a city and its surrounding countryside. Others were somewhat larger areas, where the government was in the hands of a duke, a prince, or perhaps a king. Still others were more or less "democratically" organized. That is, a local council, or senate, composed of representatives of the leading families, ruled the territory. Almost all of Europe was divided into small, often very tiny, independent states. The king of France, for example, might claim control of a large area—although not the whole of what is now France—but, in effect, he was only the nominal head of a number of small and relatively independent communities. In Germany and Italy, there was not even a nominal king.

The Holy Roman Empire was also really a fiction. In earlier days, under the great Charles, known as Charlemagne, much of central Europe had been united under one central government, although even then local independence had been a prominent factor. But with the collapse of western civilization, even before Charlemagne's time, the way had been prepared for what scholars call "fissiparation," or the breaking up of the empire. During the Dark Ages— the not entirely accurate name given to the period from about 700 or 800 A.D. to the eleventh and twelfth centuries—this breaking up had been very marked. Charlemagne had managed to arrest it, but thereafter the process went on very rapidly. The name "Holy Roman Empire" still hung on; the reality of it was otherwise.

Due to the political situation, local loyalties, and therefore, jealousies, of nearby states or cities were very marked throughout the Middle Ages. At the same time, because of many economic factors which modern scholars have analyzed and described, a movement toward national consciousness was beginning to show itself—especially during Luther's lifetime. The old feudal pattern was breaking up. In its place was emerging a mercantile society, in which the rich businessman was becoming prominent in the affairs of state. The feudal lord still existed and the local rulers were still very powerful, but the significant factor was the growing power of what we would call the "middle class." The common interests in manufacturing, buying, selling, promoting trade, developing industries, and seeking ever wider markets naturally brought people together.

Also aiding the move toward national consciousness was the growth of a sense of cultural unity. People living in Italy spoke a single language, even if there were different dialects in different parts of the peninsula. People living in the great central area of Europe spoke German. This established a kind of unity among them. And when German became a literary as well as a spoken language—when people, however few in number, began to write in that tongue as well as speak it—the drive toward national consciousness was accelerated. So, the sixteenth century was a time when Europe was still divided, yet it was also a time when the beginning of national unity was part of the life of the continent. What had happened in England a long time before now began to happen on the continent itself.

However, since national unity was only beginning, the older patterns of society continued. There were still nobles and aristocrats, many of them descendants of robber barons, local feudal lords, and others with a long history of rule. Certain groups gathered around them, forming a court with whom the ruling class could easily associate. At the other end of the social scale were the peasants, descendants of the serfs, or slaves, who had tilled the soil, done the hard work, and been owned by the overlords. They were not entirely depressed or deprived of all rights, for local laws, plus the Church's own regulations, gave them certain privileges and guaranteed that they would not be victims of too much oppression, however impoverished or illiterate they were.

In between the aristocrats and the peasants were the burghers—the townsmen, the mercantile class, and the small landowners. Hans Luther had joined this status. As a member of the lower middle class, he owned property, controlled copper foundries, and employed men. Above Hans in status were the merchants, owners of bigger industries, and men engaged in promoting commerce between the small states. This was the rising class of society.

Luther's teaching made a special appeal to the middle class. Most, although not all, of the nobles and aristocrats were content with things as they were. As for the peasants, they might break out into open revolt against what sometimes seemed intolerable

41

conditions—one such outbreak did occur during Luther's time—but on the whole, they were too much concerned with making their livelihood and were far too illiterate to take much notice of theological controversies. But the middle classes could read and write—how else could they have carried on their business activities?—and they were showing a new concern for ideas. Furthermore, they were anxious to change the existing social patterns to give themselves more control of the affairs of the world. They were not happy with the remnants of feudalism. Often, they were the moneylenders, and since they supplied the funds on which many others lived, they saw no reason why they should not have a say in government and civic matters.

Two other elements in the life of the late Middle Ages are important in the understanding of Luther and his work—education and the intellectual ferment which was called the Renaissance.

Not very many people in Luther's time attended advanced schools and universities, but in most towns of any size there were schools which, like Luther's Latin school at Mansfeld, provided the rudiments of an education. Those who attended were the children of families with a reasonably good income. Sometimes boys of peasant families were able to receive a decent education, but this was largely through the schools connected with religious houses or monasteries.

It is true that Erfurt had several thousand students, and there were famous universities with large enrollments, such as at Oxford and Cambridge in England, Paris in France, and Bologna in Italy. Yet only a few young men were able to take advantage of university instruction. Girls had no such chance, for at the time nobody thought it either necessary or proper for them to undertake advanced studies. Their place was in the home, and whatever education they received was given to them privately.

The subjects taught in the universities depended a good deal on whether the influence of the Renaissance had reached the particular institution. In Italy and England that influence had made itself known, but it had not reached most of the universities of Germany. Luther's university seems to have been very traditional. The student read the great classical authors, whose works were regarded with extraordinary reverence. He did most of his studying in Latin, even if he spoke in his native tongue outside of classes. The natural science of the time was largely a repetition of Aristotle's treatises on physics and biology. Experimental science, although it was just beginning to emerge, was not part of the curriculum. There was advanced training in mathematics and a continuation of rhetoric. The whole course of study found its peak in theology, known as "the queen of the sciences." ("Science" meant knowledge—as indicated by the Latin derivation of the word—and not what it means today.) The theology which was taught was, naturally, the official dogma of the Catholic Church. A student prepared for the study of theology through philosophy, as Martin Luther did.

All teaching was authoritative, and students were not encouraged to do much thinking for themselves. They were to learn what was in the texts, to comment on the material, and to show competence in handing it on to others. Obviously, many students did think for themselves; that is the nature of the human mind. Yet genuine independence of thought was regarded with some suspicion, especially if the new thoughts seemed in any way to question the established teaching of the Church and its official "doctors," or learned exponents.

A modern writer has said that "the entire training of home, school, and university was designed to instill the fear of God and reverence for the Church." This seems an accurate description of the education of the Middle Ages. But in places that had experienced some of the Renaissance influence, things were a little different. In those areas, a keen awareness of the rich variety of thought in the ancient world, as well as a renewed interest in man and his unique endowments, brought about more open-mindedness, a readiness to allow independence to the student, and encouragement of thought. (Erfurt was not one of those places.)

The Renaissance, or rebirth of classical culture, was once regarded as a phenomenon of the fifteenth century and thereafter. This is not quite accurate, for at times during earlier centuries, and perhaps especially during the thirteenth, there had been a reawakening to much that had been forgotten about the ancient Graeco-Roman culture. One instance was the rediscovery of the main works of Aristotle. By Luther's time, a study of Aristotle's writings had become traditional. But there was also a new awareness of much else from the ancient classical world. The Greek and later Roman writers were once again read, and some of the so-called Neoplatonic philosophers were rediscovered and studied. Coupled with this was a feeling that the accepted theology of the Church had too long minimized the capacity of men to think and to know. Nature, and man as part of nature, was important in the picture.

Martin Luther was not a Renaissance man. Of course, he was influenced by the new developments, but by and large he remained, throughout his life, a traditionalist. For him, the important thing was not the wonderful beauty of nature, much as he loved it, nor the remarkable character of the human personality in its union of body and soul. What was absolutely central for Luther was the eternal destiny of the soul—to be saved from sin and damnation, to avoid the anguish of hell, to have the assurance that one was "right with God." This was essential; everything else might be interesting, fascinating, or delightful, but it was not what really mattered. In other words, Luther was a man of his own time. His originality did not concern radical changes in the theology of the established Church but concerned man's destiny and man's hope of eternal salvation.

CHAPTER IV

In the Cloister

The day was July 2, 1505, and the warm air was heavy with humidity.

Martin Luther, recently made a Master of Arts at the University of Erfurt, was returning to the school after a visit with his parents. As Luther traveled back to the university, a storm broke, with flashes of lightning and great roars of thunder. And then, with one terrible flash, Luther was struck by a bolt of lightning and hurled to the ground. He was in terror. All his religious background, as well as his mother's superstitions about natural events and their relationship to human affairs, forced him to see the hand of God upon him. He was not physically hurt, but he had been penetrated by a sense of God's inexorable and terrible judgment.

In his terror Luther remembered Saint Anne, his father's patron saint as the heavenly guardian of miners. He cried out, "Saint Anne, save me! I will become a monk!"

The vow had been made. Young Luther rose from the ground unharmed. He had been "saved." Now he must fulfill the promise which he had made.

Like so much in Luther's life, the incident is very dramatic. It was the turning point in his life. Now he was to become more than a simple Christian believer, a layman who accepted the teachings of the Church and tried to obey the rules which the Church laid down. Now he was to devote his whole life to religion. It was to be his career, as well as the center of his existence.

Although it is easy to understand that Luther became frightened by the terrible storm, it is more difficult to grasp the profound significance with which he viewed the event. The thunderstorm, the bolt which struck him to the ground, his terror, and his vow brought to a focus a great deal more than the incident alone would suggest.

First, it must be remembered that the reality of God, the devil, the saints, heaven, hell, and purgatory was absolutely unquestioned. They were as real, as vivid, and as inescapable as a flash of lightning. God was as much a fact as a tree in the forest. The devil was no figment of the imagination but an evil spirit who intervened in the world to harm men and women and to turn them from God. The saints were real, too, and one spoke to them almost as if talking to a fellow human. Heaven was a state for which men hopefully were destined, but hell was a dreadful possibility. Purgatory was a place of cleansing and purification, and temporary punishment.

The things which happened to a man in the course of his daily life were not accidental or incidental. They did not just occur. In some mysterious way they were part of a general scheme or plan. Yet this did not suggest that men bore no personal responsibility and possessed no real freedom. On the contrary, good things occurred because God blessed the man, often through the intercession of the Virgin Mary or some other saint. Evil was a punishment for wrongdoing, or a warning to avoid that which was against the will of God. How a man exercised his freedom would determine forever whether he was to enjoy the bliss of eternal existence with God or the horror of alienation from God and interminable punishment among the damned.

So, Luther had come to think of God as an exacting and terrifying taskmaster—"God the all-terrible." Obey God or suffer the consequences. To help him obey God, a man had all the "means of grace" which the Church provided in its sacraments. He had the promise of assistance from the saints, who would pray for him in times of emergency or trouble, and, above all, he had Jesus Christ, the divine Son of God who had come into the world to save men—if only they would do what was required to make them worthy of such salvation. But Christ himself had a terrible aspect, too. In his complete holiness as the divine Son of God, he was not easily approachable except through the appointed sacramental means. Of course, there was also Christ's mother, the Virgin Mary. She was gentle and kind; she understood human nature and its defects; and she could be counted on to intercede for sinners, provided that she was invoked through sincere prayer. These were the sort of beliefs that the common people had come to entertain, often against the wishes and the teachings of so-called authorities. And these were the sort of beliefs with which young Martin Luther had been brought up.

Second, Luther had also grown up in a superstitious world. Much later, when speaking about evil, he said that "many regions are inhabited by devils." He also remarked that "in my own native land there is a high hill called Pubelsberg, on top of which is a lake. If a stone is thrown into that lake, a storm will arise over the entire area, because the waters of that lake are the abode of captive demons." If in his full maturity Luther could accept such a belief, how much more had he accepted in his youth? Religion for Luther, deep and sincere as it was, had been colored by such ideas. As he himself later said, religion for him had been very largely a matter of fear. He had been afraid of God, of God's wrath, of future punishment. Rather than releasing him from terror, his religion had increased the terror.

Finally, Luther's reaction to the thunderstorm is also interesting in terms of his personality. Most of the time he was a robust, cheerful, humorous person. But he also had moments of dreadful depression when he found himself possessed by what seemed like an evil spirit. This spirit gained control of him and plunged him into an almost death-dealing state of anxiety. In German, the word to describe this is *anfechtung*. It contains many meanings: terror, alarm, depression, gloom, hopelessness, and an inability to act constructively.

Some scholars who attack Martin Luther have taken his depressions to mean that he was mentally unhinged some of the time. Actually, he was a balanced, steady, hard worker, not a manic-depressive. Luther, an unusually sensitive genius, experienced the kind of mood changes which all of us know in some degree. In a man of genius, these moods can become extraordinarily vivid and forceful. Luther was that sort of man.

Inevitably, Luther associated his moods of depression with his religious convictions. If he felt uncontrollably disturbed, it was because the devil had got into him. He was being tempted, assaulted by evil powers, pulled down toward hell. What he needed then, above all, was a helping hand, somebody or something that would hold him steady, pull him out of the morass, reestablish his sense of security, and give him peace of mind and soul.

It was Luther's background that was largely responsible for his reaction to the storm. He had vowed to become a monk. Only in this way, he was convinced, could he find what he was seeking—"a gracious God." He was terrified of the God who could judge him. Doubtless he exaggerated the extent of his own personal sins, but he did not exaggerate his need for reassurance or his feeling that if only he could come to know God as love, he would find happiness, contentment, peace of soul, and confidence in life. Perhaps he would be able to find all that he sought in a monastery.

But first, he had to do two things. He must be accepted as a novice by a religious order, and he must inform his parents of his decision. Luther knew very well that his father would be infuriated by this disappointment of all his hopes for his son's success in a worldly profession, with a wealthy wife.

It took the young man no more than a couple of weeks to find a religious house that would accept him —the reformed Augustinian monastery in Erfurt. The discipline of the community was strict, and a novice was forced to do physical labor. During the probationary year, before he could be accepted into full membership in the order, he was obliged to satisfy his superiors that he was indeed truly "called" to the religious life. Nobody could become a full-fledged monk without this period of trial.

Luther sold his valuable copy of the *Corpus Juris,* and he entertained his university friends at a farewell party, where he ate and drank for the last time as a "man of the world." Thereafter, so far as he knew, he would live entirely cloistered from the world. When he arrived at the monastery, he was taken to the resident head, the prior, who gave him a place in the guesthouse until the proper inquiries could be made. One such inquiry, of course, went to Hans Luther. As predicted, the old man was horrified by his son's act. The boy who had been his pride and joy, and would have been the support of his old age, was leaving the family, and the father had no patience with him. Yet the son, now almost twenty-two, was old enough to make his own decision, and there was nothing that the parents could do about it. Hans was bitter, and he would not forgive his son for some time. (Only when two other sons later died did Hans give his unwilling, almost surly, consent. Some of Hans' friends told him that the deaths must be accepted as divine judgment on his refusal to give his oldest son to the "way of perfection" which the religious life offered.)

The service at which Luther was accepted as a novice was very impressive. It included the promise that thereafter he would be entirely obedient to the requirements of his religious superiors. He would fast, observe the austerities which were part of the rule, overcome the desires of the flesh, participate in all the worship of the community, and share entirely in the common life of the order. He would spend his first year in prayer and in the reading of the Holy Scriptures. He would discipline his body and would refuse all luxuries. His cell was a tiny cubicle, perhaps six by nine feet, furnished with only a rough cot and a prayer desk.

All went well. Presumably Luther was not only faithful to his vows, but he felt at peace in his soul. Furthermore, because he was obviously a promising young man, those in charge arranged for him to prepare himself for the priesthood. He was assigned books which dealt with the dogmas of the Church, and he carefully studied a famous exposition of the meaning of the mass written by Gabriel Biel, a follower of the Ockhamist tradition and a distinguished philosophical theologian. This book confirmed the philosophical ideas which Luther already had accepted as a student, and it also filled him with deep reverence for the mystery of the mass.

When he was not praying, attending services which lasted for hours each day, or studying, Luther could enjoy the friendship of other members of the community, although talk was permitted for only a brief time each day. In his later days Luther said that during the first year a man spends in a monastery "the devil is silent."

The day of Luther's first celebration of the mass began auspiciously. Hans, although still not entirely happy about his son's decision, came to Erfurt to be present at the service. He arrived with some twenty horsemen and a gift of money which would go to the monastery. Perhaps Hans thought that he could make some recompense for the inner distaste which he felt about his son's decision. For young Luther, the celebration was a terrifying experience. The mass was a sacred rite, in which (according to the belief of the Catholic Church) the bread and wine on the altar were changed (transubstantiated) into the body and blood of Christ. Their outward appearance was not changed, but their significance was now truly the spiritual reality of Christ himself. In consecrating the elements of bread and wine, the priest was God's agent working a tremendous miracle. He must be in a state of grace, having confessed his sins and received absolution. He must be meticulous in performing the proper ritual actions, the various gestures, the sign of the cross, and other requirements of the rite as prescribed in the Church's canons and in the "rubrics," or directions for the celebration.

Luther managed to get through the service, but he

had once again experienced *anfechtung*—that combination of dread, fear, despair, and hopelessness about himself and his unworthiness, even though he was in the state of grace which the Church required. When it was all over, he went to join his father and other guests at a meal. Luther had purposely arranged to celebrate his first mass on a day that his father could attend. He wished to have a renewed understanding and to have Hans' assurance that the older man had accepted his decision. Luther had not seen his father since he had left home on the return trip to Erfurt. Now all would be well.

But the old man was incensed when his son spoke to him. He did not wish to be treated—as it seemed to him that his son was doing—as if he, the father, had made a great mistake and must now acknowledge his error. Hans indignantly told his son that God had commanded that father and mother were to be honored, and now his son had left them both "to look after ourselves alone when we get old." Hans did not stop there, for when Luther pointed out that his decision had been brought about by divine intervention and the call experienced during the thunderstorm, the old man replied, "Well, may God grant that it was not an appearance of the devil to you."

Hans went home, still not happy with his son. Luther continued in the monastery, deeply distressed by his father's attitude. Nonetheless, he was exemplary in the vigor and devotion with which he carried on his new duties as a priest. In speaking of this period, he said that he had been a "bondslave" of the mass, because he brought the sacrament to lay people and also because there was great benefit to the priest himself from celebrating the mass. Luther believed that the more masses he could say, the more prayers and austerities he could engage in, the closer he would be to the salvation of his soul. And this, above all, was what he was seeking.

Luther's religious superiors not only saw in him a person of much promise but also recognized that he would make an excellent teacher in their order. So they made the necessary arrangements for him to be admitted to advanced study, leading to the degree of Doctor of Theology. He began this work at once and showed great ability in the university lecture courses and in the required reading. He showed such ability that, in 1508, he went to the university at Wittenberg to spend the semester lecturing on moral philosophy, or the study of the principles of Christian conduct, and also giving courses in the Bible. The following year he returned to Erfurt, where he resumed his studies in his own monastery, at the same time assisting in university lectures on *The Sentences* of Peter Lombard. This book was one of the great theological texts of the day. Students would read portions of it before each lecture, and then the teacher would expound on the meaning of the passages and show how the differing ideas which Lombard had collected could be reconciled in Christian dogma.

In 1510, Luther made a visit to Rome, the headquarters of the Church, and the place of residence of the pope.

The trip was not Luther's own choice. He was sent along with another priest, to make representations on a matter that was very important to the German Augustinian community. The Augustinians were divided into two main groups. One of them (to which the Erfurt congregation belonged) followed the prescribed rules very strictly, while the other tended to be a bit more relaxed in observance. A plan had been proposed to unite all Augustinians into one great congregation. The proposal had the support of the authorities in Rome and was also approved by Johannes von Staupitz, the vicar general of the German Augustinians, a man of both holiness and common sense. But opposition to the project was vigorous, in Erfurt and elsewhere. The purpose of the trip was to present strong arguments against any unification that might lead all congregations of the order to accept a more lax observance of the rules.

The journey did not have the official approval of the vicar general, and as a matter of fact little was accomplished by it. The proposal for complete unification of the German congregations was eventually dropped because opposition was so strong. As far as

Luther was concerned, the great significance of the trip was the opportunity to visit Rome itself.

He stayed there for about a month. During this time, when not engaged in Church business, he toured the great city. He said afterward that he had seen all the churches which he could crowd into his stay, had gone to all the holy monuments, had seen the enormous number of relics which were on display, and had "gone the rounds" like a pilgrim. Above all, he had gained for himself the merit which was promised to all the faithful who visited the holy city. This meant that for every sacred spot visited, shrine inspected, or relic reverenced, a certain amount of credit was put down for the pilgrim. This credit would not guarantee him any heavenly reward, but it would be applied against the penances or penalties which his sins accumulated in this world. Gaining merit in this way was part of the pattern of the times.

To be in Rome, the city where the pope and the leaders of the Church had their headquarters, was thrilling for Luther, but once or twice he was disconcerted. When he celebrated mass, slowly and with great reverence, the Italians were amused and diverted. They said, *Passa, passa*—"hurry up with it." And once, when crawling up the famous Scala Sancta, still to be seen across the piazza from the Basilica of San Giovanni in Laterano which is the cathedral church of the diocese of Rome, he found himself wondering if the exercise was worthwhile. It was said that if a person climbed the steps on his knees, kissing each step and murmuring a prayer, he could free some soul from the pains of purgatory. Luther did this for his grandfather, but when he got to the top, he thought to himself, "Who knows whether all this is really true?"

Luther was also worried by the gossip in Rome about the scandalously immoral and indecently luxurious lives of the leading clergy. Not too long before, Pope Alexander VI had quite openly had mistresses and had often behaved in a shocking fashion. And some high dignitaries still behaved shockingly. The simple piety and austere morality of the German monk was offended and shocked by what he heard. He knew perfectly well that, according to the sound Catholic theology which he accepted, the wickedness of popes and priests could not diminish the benefits which Christ wished to bestow through his Church on earth. Nonetheless, Luther found it very difficult to reconcile such behavior with the high responsibility attached to the sacerdotal office.

His visit to Rome was another critical occasion in Luther's life. He was still a faithful and pious Catholic believer and a devoted priest; yet he was deeply troubled by the appalling laxity of those who were at the very center of the ecclesiastical institution. And he was also beginning to have some questions about the value of the things which he had so far accepted without question—such matters as the reverence given to relics and the possibility of acquiring merit.

When Luther returned to Erfurt, von Staupitz—who evidently liked the young man and felt that he needed careful watching as well as fatherly assistance—called him to Wittenberg once again. He appointed Luther as preacher to the monks at the "Black Cloister" (the Augustinians wore black habits). He also made Luther a teacher of biblical studies and gave him the post of subprior in the Wittenberg house. This was a position of great responsibility, for it involved giving instructions to novices in the order. Perhaps von Staupitz felt that it would do Luther good to have such responsibility.

The young man also continued his studies at Wittenberg, and in October, 1512, he received the degree of Doctor of Theology. This meant that he was now an honored scholar, an officially recognized teacher in theology. He would be able not only to assist in lectures, as he had done previously, or offer relatively simple survey courses, but he could lecture to students who would consider him their authority.

So, at the age of twenty-nine, Dr. Martin Luther began his work in the town of Wittenberg, a village with perhaps twenty-five hundred inhabitants. In August, 1516, he began his lectures at the university, taking the Psalms as his subject. At the end of that year, and in 1517, he lectured on Saint Paul's letters

to the Romans and the Galatians. He was still a
monk, and still lived in a cloister, but his new work
and new duties now brought him to the point where
he was forced to make what has been called "the
Lutheran theological breakthrough."

Chapter V

The Discovery of the Gospel

Martin Luther's "breakthrough" was his discovery of the authentic Christian gospel. And with it came the discovery which he phrased in classical theological terms: "justification by grace through faith only." This apparently complicated phrase represents the contribution which the German Reformer made to the Christianity in which he so firmly believed. His discoveries brought about the division of the Christian world into Catholic and

Protestant. Yet today, these same two points have become the means by which the divided Christian groups are now finding it possible to come together again in sympathy and brotherhood.

What led Luther to discover—actually to rediscover—the authentic Christian gospel? How did he come to insist on justification?

Luther, as we know, was seeking inner security, peace of soul, and the sense that he was accepted and loved by God. One of the ways in which he tried to obtain these things was through extreme personal austerity. He engaged in long fasts, abstaining from all food for days on end. He spent hours in prayer, going through all the prescribed forms and doing much more than the rules of his order required. Sometimes he spent winter nights without blankets, thinking that by thus disciplining his body he could find peace of soul.

There was hardly a method which he did not try. He later said about himself, "I was a good monk and I kept the rule of my order so strictly that I may say that if a monk ever got into heaven through following his 'monkery' it was I. . . . If I had kept on much longer, I should have killed myself with vigils, prayers, reading, and other work."

The clue to Luther's mistake at that period of his life is the word—"work." Luther believed, as did so many people of his time, that a person could work his way into the security, peace, and assurance which he desired. It might be said that his basic error was in assuming that one can buy love. For it was love that Luther wanted—not so much to be able to love, but rather to have the certainty that he was loved, loved by God. Luther failed to realize that love is never earned simply because one has tried hard to merit it. A song says, "You can't buy love with money"; the truth is, you can't buy love at all.

The great Church theologians had never said that anyone could earn love, but the way in which their views had been explained to the average man during the Middle Ages suggested exactly the opposite. Therefore, it was thought by many, including priests, monks, nuns, and other official churchmen, that pious works—prayers, vigils, fastings, pilgrimages, etc.—would win the bliss of heaven, avert the perils of hell, and secure inner peace.

But perhaps there were other things that one could do to attain one's desire. It was the accepted belief that sins could be forgiven only through confessing them to a priest and receiving absolution, or a declaration of God's pardon. If Luther's sense of alienation and his lack of peace were the result of sin, then he would confess his sins again and again. And he did so. He made enormous lists of his wrongdoings, usually little peccadilloes (as he later admitted), for he was not a man of gross nature. He wore out his confessor with his continual dwelling on sin—so much so that he was once told that he was simply hunting for wrongs to confess. A contemporary Catholic theologian has said that the danger in what is a good and helpful practice—namely, private confession—is that it will encourage the penitent to "engage in a spiritual flea-hunt." Certainly this was the case with Luther. The more he confessed, the more he found to confess. He almost manufactured sins so that he might secure the benefit of absolution. His adviser and friend, von Staupitz, told him that he was guilty of scrupulosity and that he did not really seem to have confidence in God's love for him. God would love Luther even if he forgot to confess some little mistaken thought which he regarded as sinful.

The difference, of course, was that von Staupitz knew God's love. But Luther felt that he did not know it. When he was told that he should follow the pattern of the great saints and simply let himself sink in God's love for him, he was entirely unable to do so. For could he be certain that God's innermost nature *is* love?

As we know, the common man in those days thought of God as the terrible judge, and Christ the divine Son as unapproachable by men. The kind of faith Luther had known as a child and young man did not emphasize the love of God. On the contrary, it stressed God's wrath against man the wicked sinner, and it spoke of ways in which that wrath could be appeased. This was actually a perversion of the true gospel, which Luther discovered when he studied the books of the New Testament for his lectures at Wittenberg.

Luther was a busy university teacher, and in demand as a preacher. In one year he delivered more than one hundred and seventy sermons. He had already taught a course on Genesis, the first book of the Bible, and now he was to lecture on the Psalms. He was popular and respected as a lecturer. His students saw that he was a good scholar and they recognized his ability to communicate what he had learned. Luther was not content to work from the accepted Latin text of the Bible. He learned Hebrew, to be able to read the Old Testament in its original, and Greek, to be able to do the same with the New Testament. His colleague, Johannes Lang, a distinguished linguistic expert on the faculty of the University of Wittenberg, helped him. Through Lang, Luther also met George Spalatin, and this acquaintanceship was later to be important to him.

Spalatin was soon named secretary to Prince Frederick, a good ruler who was called "Frederick the Wise." He was an elector of the Holy Roman Empire, one of the petty princes who formed the council of the widespread imperium. Frederick was the head of the area which included Wittenberg, and he was a vigorous supporter of the university. Indeed, Frederick was very proud of this relatively recent institution. He wished to make it the rival of such famous German universities as Leipzig. In order to do this, he had secured the support of the Augustinian and Franciscan orders. It was through their help that he obtained young and competent professors, among them Martin Luther himself.

Luther was doing more than teaching, however. He was preaching in the Town Church at Wittenberg, as the subprior of the cloister there. In 1515, von Staupitz had named him district vicar of the Augustinian order. This is an indication of Luther's ability and of the confidence which his superiors felt in him. As district vicar he had control of eleven houses of the Augustinians in the district around Wittenberg. Furthermore, he was respected as an authority on matters of theology and ethics. Hence, a good deal of his time was spent in counseling and advising.

Through his work as preacher and counselor, as administrator and lecturer, Luther was brought face to face with the practical problems of the Church. As a result his own problems were complemented by the recognition that all was not well with the Church itself. It became very clear to Luther that in many quarters religion was regarded as a business matter. In order to support the Church, to maintain its buildings, and to obtain funds for the completion of the new Saint Peter's in Rome, many of those in charge adopted methods of raising money that seemed doubtful if not entirely wrong.

One such method was the sale of indulgences. Albert of Brandenburg, a member of the ruling Hohenzollern family, had been given two bishoprics when he was far too young, in terms of the ecclesiastical law, to hold any such office. But Albert aspired to the archbishopric of Mainz. If he were given it, he would be the ecclesiastical head of all Germany. To secure the post, he would be obliged to pay the fee of ten thousand ducats, which he did not have and could not raise. So, negotiations were started between Albert and the Roman curia through a German banking house, famous for its money-lending, and well in control of the Church's finances in Germany.

It was finally agreed that the ten thousand ducats would be paid, but the method of raising the money would be through the sale of indulgences in the territories over which Albert would have control. Such a sale would continue for a period of eight years. The sale was not permitted in Wittenberg itself, since Prince Frederick would not allow it. Yet people from there could easily cross the borders into adjacent areas and buy indulgences. The proclamation of this fantastic commercial operation was in the hands of a Dominican monk named Tetzel.

What were these indulgences? The theory was that when a man's sins were forgiven, through confession, he still must make some "satisfaction" for the wrongs he had done. "Acts of contrition" were prescribed

69

as penalties for sins by the priest who heard the confession. They were intended to demonstrate the absolute sincerity of the penitent. Such penalties, it was thought, could be reduced or even entirely waived, if the Church so decided. The official teaching stated that only the penalties that the Church had imposed could be reduced or removed. But the ordinary man or woman assumed that the granting of an indulgence (removing or reducing the penality) meant that actual forgiveness by God was available —at a price. If a simple peasant paid the proper amount, he could be guaranteed eternal salvation.

Crowds of people followed Tetzel as he went about proclaiming the value of indulgences. Whatever Tetzel himself may have thought, the evil aspect of the enterprise was apparent, and Luther had to deal with this problem. Was it right to sell such things, when almost certainly the simple folk would misunderstand? Luther was not questioning, at the moment, the Christian validity of indulgences. His concern was only with the commercial nature of the business and with the way in which uneducated and superstitious people were being misled. As people came to him for confession, he realized that they believed they could receive forgiveness simply because they had purchased the paper which granted an indulgence. This would not do, and Luther was forced to examine the matter very carefully.

By now, Luther was used to examining matters

carefully. For some time, he had been carefully studying the books of the New Testament in order to
prepare his lectures. And when he began to study
the letters of Saint Paul to the Romans and the
Galatians, he found something that he had not previously understood. The terrible God of judgment is
not the real God at all. The real God is sheer love
and goodness. He only appears to be terrible, and He
appears this way only to men who cannot recognize
that, in their sinful condition, they are not ready to
accept Him as love. Jesus Christ had come into the
world to disclose to everybody that the heart of God
is "pure unbounded love." And the gospel, which
contains the whole meaning of Christianity, is
nothing other than the announcement that God is
love, love disclosed in the whole life of Jesus, especially in the willingness of Jesus to die so that men
can see how far love will go to help those who need
desperately to know its meaning.

God only appears to be terrible and full of wrath
and anger. His real character and true nature is loving and gracious. This He has shown in "sending
Jesus Christ into the world." Whether men are sinners or not, God loves them and will always love
them. That is the basic truth of the Christian gospel.
That is why there *is* Christianity—to tell men, to
show men, to help them understand and accept God's
love.

With this discovery, Luther made another. The

usual theological description of it is "justification by grace through faith only." What does that mean? No amount of pious acts, no number of pilgrimages, no accumulation of merit, however obtained, will give men the inner security, the peace of mind and soul, or the assurance that they want and need. Only one thing will give this to them: their full acceptance of the reality of God's love for them. And they can do this in but one way—by having utter and absolute trust in God, who is revealed in Christ as love. Once this acceptance is central in their lives, they need no longer fear God. They can and must love Him, because they know that He loves them, accepts them as they are, and will do everything possible to help them become true, full, and complete people.

In Luther's own words, spoken much later at Heidelberg, he had discovered that "the love of God which lives in men loves sinners . . . in order to make them live righteously. The love of God does not seek its own good, but it flows out and bestows good on His children. Therefore, sinners are not attractive people who are loved by God; they are loved by God and then they are attractive." God does not love us because we are good people; we become good people when we respond to His love for us. Luther had been seeking "a gracious God." Now he had found Him. As he himself so often said, God in His love had sought *him*—as He sought every man—and God had found him, Martin Luther. In that fact, he—and every man—could rest secure, with peace in his heart, and with the assurance that nothing "could separate him from the love of God which was in Christ Jesus our Lord." Those words, from the last verse of Chapter 8 of Paul's letter to the Romans, provided for Luther the answer to his restlessness. Once and for all, fear of God as a terrible judge was removed. Luther could live freely and happily, if only he placed all his trust in that love of God.

Luther had come to see all this because he had worked hard on the New Testament for his lectures, but the tragedy was that he had not known it long before. Later on, he would find comfort in another New Testament phrase, this time from the first letter of Saint John: "There is no fear in love, for perfect love casts out fear." It may seem strange that with all of Luther's familiarity with the Bible, both as a young novice and later as a teacher, such texts had not dawned upon him. But now they had fully dawned upon him. And Martin Luther reached an entirely new and wonderful grasp of Christianity.

This discovery of the authentic gospel, coupled with the understanding of how it works in men (justifying them by grace through faith alone), is the Lutheran breakthrough. And it helps us to see why Luther became so impatient with the whole matter of indulgences. He saw clearly that eternal salvation and forgiveness of sins must rest only on the gospel promise, on the assurance of God as love, and on nothing else.

So, after examining the matter of indulgences very carefully, Luther drew up his famous "Ninety-Five Theses on the Power and Efficacy of Indulgences." On All Saints' Day, October 31, 1517, he nailed the Theses on the door of the Castle Church at Wittenberg.

Almost immediately, an enormous controversy broke out. Luther was still a faithful Catholic, convinced that what he had discovered was the truth which the Church really intended to teach, and so the controversy was entirely within the Church. It was not as if Luther had in any way separated himself from the institutional Church, although in the light of later events, he did feel obliged to leave it. But even then, he and his followers believed that they were working for a purified and reformed Christian community. They were not starting an entirely new religious institution.

Luther's Theses began by stating frankly, in the light of his own new experience, that the whole life of man should be one of repentance for failure to do God's will. Purchasing an indulgence was a dangerous thing, not only because it encouraged mistaken ideas but also because the money could be much better used to look after the needy and the sick. Luther agreed that the pope and the appointed clergy can remit, remove, or reduce penalties which they themselves have imposed—that is, such acts as the Church may from time to time require of the truly penitent. But it is entirely wrong to think, Luther declared, that the pope or the clergy can do anything about what God has imposed or required. Therefore, "souls in purgatory" cannot be helped by the buying of indulgences on their behalf. As for those still alive, no indulgences are needed to secure God's forgiveness. God is gracious and loving, and He forgives the sins and mistakes of everybody who turns to Him in genuine faith and with true sorrow for wrongs done.

This was Luther's new discovery at work in a practical way. But what he said contradicted what was taken by many lay people and clergy to be the official line of the Church's teaching. The Theses were soon translated from the Latin in which Luther had written them and were circulated (not by Luther's own direct intention) all over the German homeland. They were given a mixed reception. Those who felt strongly that people of German speech and culture must stand together—in what might be described as a new national unity—looked at them as a kind of "manifesto" against the way in which German money was being drained off to Rome, through the sale of indulgences, to pay for a great Roman church building. Many lay people, who had long been resentful of what they took to be an overpowering churchly control of men's lives, thought that the Theses were the beginning of a movement for human freedom. Among Church leaders, however, the reaction was very different. Here was a direct challenge to them, as well as an onslaught on what had been a profitable enterprise raising vast sums of money.

Albert of Brandenburg was naturally incensed. He asked the theologians of his own University of Mainz to give him an opinion, but they refused, telling him to put the question to the pope. Pope Leo X is reported to have said, "Luther is a drunken German. He will feel different when he is sober."

It is doubtful that the Pope really did say this, just as it is doubtful that he said, "That Friar Martin is a brilliant chap, and the whole fuss in Germany is due to the envy of the monks." As for others in the Church, they charged that Luther was really attacking something other than indulgences. He was, they said, criticizing the powers of the papacy itself. Hence, he was to be regarded as a heretic. Dr. Johann Eck, who had been a friend of Luther's, went so far as to publish a pamphlet saying that Luther was teaching ideas like those which John Hus, the Bohemian leader of some decades before, had taught. And Hus had been burned at the stake for his heresy, so Luther had better watch out. The Dominicans, the order to which Tetzel belonged, were infuriated.

Soon there was enough opposition to make it plain that Luther's life might actually be endangered.

The Theses had been published in 1517, four years before the meeting at Worms. During those four years Martin did not behave like a man leading a furious attack on the Church. And he did not think of himself as such. He continued his teaching and preaching, carried on his duties in the Wittenberg church, and busied himself with such local concerns as finding a suitable professor of Hebrew for Prince Frederick's University at Wittenberg. However, there were important incidents during the four-year period, including a remarkable one at Heidelberg, where Luther went for the regular triennial chapter of the Augustinian order. He expected to be badly treated, even to find his life threatened, but to his amazement he was invited to dinner by the Count Palatine, ruler of the area. Luther found himself taken as the leader of a movement of "angry young men," who had a cause. Some of those who would later be leaders of the Reformation, once it had really made its start, were also present: John Brenz, later the reforming priest of Würtemberg; and Martin Bucer, who became the leader of the reform in Strassburg.

One other incident was not of Luther's making. Tetzel wrote a defense of the sale of indulgences, and copies of his document reached Wittenberg.

Some eight hundred copies were collected in the town, and an enthusiastic group of students at the university made a great public bonfire of them. Luther had nothing to do with this, nor did the Prince Elector Frederick or the authorities of the university. Indeed, Luther felt much embarrassment at this impetuous act, however much he may have appreciated the support of the young men.

Luther did not bother to reply to Tetzel's defense, but he did write an explanation of the Theses and permitted sermons that he had preached to be circulated. In this way he hoped to keep the record straight. He brought out one point very clearly—the mistranslation of a text in Scripture upon which much popular teaching had been based. In Matthew's Gospel, Chapter 4, Verse 17, the Latin text reads *penitentium agite* ("do penance") for the original Greek phrase which means simply, "change your mind" or "be a penitent person."

These and other matters finally brought a summons for Luther to go to Rome and appear before the authorities there. He was given sixty days to obey the order. Luther felt that the trip would be highly dangerous for him, and he asked Prince Frederick to see that any trial that he might have to face would be held in Germany and not in Rome. But before anything had to be done, the pope changed his mind. A new order was sent from Rome, directing that Luther was to be arrested immediately and to appear before Cardinal Cajetan, the papal representative in Germany.

Luther had come to know Spalatin, Prince Frederick's secretary and court chaplain, and the friendship became the means of averting the threatened arrest. Through Spalatin, Prince Frederick was persuaded to grant Luther protection as a loyal subject in his realm. He was also persuaded to reject the idea of Luther's arrest and to ask that a trial be held in Germany, with a fair chance given the young monk to state his case. Cajetan agreed to this, and Luther went to the city of Augsburg to discuss the situation with the Cardinal. The interview ended unhappily, for during the discussion it became clear that Luther was not sticking to his original position. Further studies had led him to feel that claims were made for the papacy which were biblically and historically unfounded. The papacy *could* make mistakes; it *had* made them. Even past Church councils had erred. This meant that Luther was now questioning basic Catholic dogma.

Cajetan urged Frederick to turn "this Wittenberg heretic" over to the designated religious authorities or to expel him from his own territory so that he could be arrested elsewhere. Frederick refused. He wanted a fair trial, and he sent to Rome asking for a document which would list precisely what were thought to be the errors and heresies of his young professor. Then Luther could be guaranteed a chance to answer. If he were a heretic, it would become apparent at the trial. But the Prince did not wish condemnation with no chance for reply.

However, a papal bull (or brief document) demanding Luther's recantation was issued in the summer of 1520. He was given sixty days to submit. Meanwhile, he had engaged in a debate with Dr. Eck; he had published several pamphlets; and he had been told that in Cologne a bonfire had been made of his books as heretical and anti-Catholic. He had also been offered protection from all physical harm by a band of one hundred knights who wished to support him. These young men, influenced by the Renaissance movement, saw in Luther one of themselves, a person who stood for human dignity and freedom.

A few of Luther's writings during this period are notable and have become very famous. One of these is called *Address to the German Nobility*. In this booklet he appealed to the nobility and aristocracy of Germany to support their own people against all attempts made to control them from outside. A second was *The Babylonian Captivity of the Church*, in which Luther urged that the Catholic Church itself was in error. He frankly charged that the way in which the sacramental system of the Church was operated was blasphemous and a denial of the meaning of the gospel. Baptism and the Holy Communion, or mass, were the only real biblical sacraments.

Private confession might be a useful practice, but it was not scripturally commanded. Indeed, Luther said the whole structure of sacramental teaching was the attempt of ecclesiastics to control the lives of Christian men and women.

The third writing, *The Freedom of the Christian Man*, was a clear statement of Luther's conviction that every believer must follow his own conscience, that he is free from dependence upon all humanly devised rules (such as Luther said the Church's regulations had turned out to be), and that the truth about Christian life could be stated in the following way: "A Christian is a perfectly free lord of all, subject to none; yet a Christian is a perfectly dutiful servant of all, subject to all." Every Christian is "free" because he is the child of God whom God loves, but, on the other hand, every Christian is obliged, by that very love of God for him, to be the servant of all men.

It is clear enough that with the publication of these tracts and booklets, as well as by his plain statements to Cajetan and others, Luther had put himself in the position of spokesman for more than mere criticism of the Church. He was now speaking out about the profound errors of the ecclesiastical institution as he saw them. In doing so, he was speaking for himself and for many others. In his own university, the Lutheran movement (as it was now beginning to be called) was strongly supported by a number of people—not least the moderate and learned Philip Melanchthon, who before long became Luther's closest colleague and collaborator.

One incident symbolizes the whole development, and Melanchthon was associated with it. Acting on Luther's behalf, he gathered students and faculty at Wittenberg for a great meeting at the Elster Gate of the city. There, as a reprisal for the burning of Luther's books at Cologne, a whole mass of books was thrown into a bonfire, including papal constitutions, works of canon law (or the requirements set forth by ecclesiastical officials), books of theology which taught what (they believed) Luther had shown to be false, the writings of Johann Eck in defense of indulgences, and others. Luther himself threw into the blazing fire the papal bull which had called him to account. When it was all over, the students paraded about town singing the hymn *Te Deum* ("We Praise Thee, O God"), with which God traditionally was thanked for his goodness.

That blaze in the little university town of Wittenberg symbolized the larger blaze which this German monk—then only thirty-seven years old—had kindled in Europe.

CHAPTER VI

After the
Diet of Worms

It was inevitable that Luther should be called
before the council of the Holy Roman Empire. Re-
ligiously speaking, Germany was afire. The official
Church was outraged by this young German monk.
Support for his movement for reform was coming
from many quarters, and it seemed that internal
revolution threatened. The merchant class was now
profoundly influenced; noblemen were forced to take
sides for or against Lutheran ideas. In the universi-

ties, students were following the Lutheran line and many of the teachers were indicating their support of Luther in their lectures. Something had to be done.

After Luther made his bold reply to the council at Worms, a specifically Lutheran variety of Christianity had emerged. Not that Luther approved of calling it by his name. For him it was simply Evangelical Christianity, which means Gospel Christianity. The word *evangel* is the Greek for "gospel." In Europe most modern Lutherans, especially in Germany, call themselves by the name Luther wished to be used, Evangelicals—gospel men.

A few days after his refusal to recant his beliefs, Luther left the city of Worms. He went to the castle known as Wartburg where he remained in seclusion for some months to avoid any possibility of arrest by the authorities of the Holy Roman Empire or the Church. Meanwhile, on May 8, 1521, an edict was ready for publication. It was decided to condemn Luther. Young Charles V, the Holy Roman Emperor, had made his own position entirely clear. "A lone friar who goes against all Christianity for a thousand years must be wrong," the emperor told the electors at the diet. "After hearing his obstinant defense yesterday, I must say that I regret having so long delayed taking action against this man for heresy. I will have nothing more to do with him. He may return with a safe-conduct, but he must not preach or make any disturbance. And I will proceed against him as a notorious heretic."

Of the electors, four out of six signed a statement agreeing with the emperor. The two who did not sign were Ludwig of the Palatinate and Prince Frederick of Saxony. Frederick had not agreed with Luther but he had respected him. Now he absolutely refused to have anything to do with what he believed to be an unfair and prejudiced attack on the young monk.

The edict of condemnation was not published at once. Prepared by Alexander, the nuncio of the pope, it was a bitter document, charging Luther with an incredible list of crimes. He "has sullied marriage, disparaged confession, denied the 'body and blood' of the Lord." It accused him of making sacraments purely subjective. It declared that his "teaching makes for rebellion, division, war, murder, robbery, arson, and the collapse of Christendom. . . . He does more harm to the civil than to the ecclesiastical authority." The edict was so worded that it made the monk of Wittenberg appear almost a devil. And it cleverly insinuated that should his opinions not be condemned, and the man himself not apprehended and punished, revolution would break out in all the states and principalities of Germany, perhaps in the whole of Europe.

The edict was published on May 26, more than a month after Luther's speech. It was approved by only a part of the diet itself, for many of those who had been present had long since gone to their own homes.

Many more Germans than even the Church may have believed, and than the emperor thought probable, rallied to Luther's support. This was the beginning of the separation between those who would maintain the established interpretation of the Christian faith and those who would follow Luther's interpretation.

Through all this, Luther remained at Wartburg, disguised as a German knight. He had been given the name of Junker George, and had been trained in the manners of a German nobleman. He had stayed in his room in the fortress until his monk's tonsure disappeared. He now wore long hair and had grown a beard. All this was according to a plan made by Frederick of Saxony.

As soon as Frederick had realized that Luther's case was lost—so far as the secular and religious authorities were concerned—he had made arrangements for Luther to be "kidnapped" while supposedly on his way back to Wittenberg. A group of knights, chosen by Frederick, intercepted the young monk, took him captive (as it was to be claimed), and hurried him off through the Thuringian forest to Wartburg. Once Frederick had decided to commit himself to Luther's support, he was prepared to carry to the limit his assurance that the young monk would be protected.

Alone in the castle with only a few servants around him, Luther began to realize the meaning of all that he had said and done, the meaning of the response which he had received from numbers of nobles and aristocrats, from members of the middle classes, and from the simple uneducated German people. For him, this was a terrible time of testing. Could he be wrong? Was he being proud and contentious? Was he fooling himself and those who listened to him and now wished to follow him? Was all this business nothing but the assault of the devil, seeking to undo the entire Christian faith and ruin the Christian civilization of Europe?

These moods of depression and hopelessness came again and again. He was possessed by his *anfechtung,* his deep inner anxiety, his awful internal agony. Was God really with him or was he (Luther) entirely deluded? This was not a new experience for Luther, and he worked his way out of it by occupying himself with an enormous amount of labor. Letters, sermons, tracts, and devotional meditations poured from his pen. What was most important of all, he began to translate the New Testament into German. Before this, only bits of the sacred books had been translated, but now he was determined to make the whole New Testament available in the language of the ordinary German. It is astounding that Luther was able to complete the translation in less than three months, working night and day.

Luther's life was marked by dramatic incidents, and one of these occurred at Wartburg. He was working one day, not entirely recovered from his depression and worry. As he wrote, it seemed to him that the devil appeared in person and began to taunt him. Luther picked up an inkwell and hurled it at the unwelcome visitor. The inkwell struck the wall, staining it, and the devil disappeared. Even today, visitors to the castle are shown the spot which the ink discolored. Perhaps in Luther's emotional state, and with his strong conviction of the reality of divine and demonic powers, he projected the vision from his inner consciousness. It was certainly real enough to him. But the devil could not deflect him from the work he was doing. And that is the important thing about this remarkable man of genius. However outlandish some of these incidents may seem—the bolt of lightning, the apparition of the devil—the fact is that Luther pursued his course, completed his work, and accomplished his reformation. He was a man of his age, to whom such things as appearances of the devil were no figments of the imagination but were vivid and real.

Although Luther himself had disappeared—some even thought that he was dead—in his own town and university his reform was proceeding. A whole series of events occurred, many of which Luther might not have desired. For example, on September 22, 1521, Melanchthon, Luther's friend and fellow professor, celebrated an "evangelical" Lord's Supper in the town. Two months later, thirteen of the monks in the Augustinian cloister decided to leave that religious house. A month later, Andreas Carlstadt, another professor and archdeacon of the Castle Church —the doctor who had conferred Luther's degree— for the first time gave the wine of the Holy Communion to the laity.

Indeed, during the time that Luther was at Wartburg and in the period shortly after his return to Wittenberg, the practical consequences of his theological affirmations began to accumulate. The rapidity with which they occurred was astounding. And the ordinary German, who had sympathized with what Luther was trying to do in curbing the overlordship of the clerics and in advocating the freedom of the Christian man, now saw that when the new understanding of the gospel and the emphasis on acceptance by God through "faith only" were taken seriously, nothing was left untouched in the old established ways of Christian worship, prayer, and life. Some were horrified, but many rejoiced.

The common man saw that parts of the mass were now being put into German, masses for the dead were discontinued in many churches, meat was eaten on the old fast days, monks and nuns left their religious houses, clerics took wives, and church buildings had some of their statues removed. Here was nothing theoretical but something visible and plain. The clergy who had taken Luther for their leader were now carrying out what they believed to be the implications of his views.

When Luther heard that several priests—including Dr. Carlstadt—had been married, he was pleased. Yet he himself did not think of marriage, and in one of his letters he expressed himself forcibly, saying, "Will the people at Wittenberg give wives to monks? Well, they won't give one to me!"

The marriage of the clergy was a natural result of Luther's insistence that the common life of ordinary people was blessed by God, entirely "holy" if those who lived it did so in faith and repentance and because they sought to serve God and their fellowmen in this fashion. There was nothing especially holy about taking the old monastic vows and trying to "get to God" in some unusual manner. Luther wrote a treatise on the subject, saying that he was glad that he had become a monk since he had learned through experience that there is no need to adopt the religious life instead of the ordinary secular one. All Christians are called to do their work, whatever it is, for God's sake and for the help of their brethren. Marriage is a good thing, he insisted; there is nothing in Holy Scripture to show that monasticism is particularly pleasing to God. When this treatise was published, many monks and nuns felt free to leave their communities. Luther's Augustinian order at Wittenberg held a meeting of the leaders to discuss the question of monastic vows. They decided that any member of the order, from that time on, was free to remain or to leave, as his conscience dictated.

Luther made a brief visit, in disguise, to Wittenberg in December of 1521. He had heard very disquieting reports about what was going on in the town. Practically all the members of the university were now avowed Lutherans; so were many of the townspeople. Luther had heard that under Carlstadt and others the most extreme changes were being made, sometimes in a disorderly way. His brief visit reassured him. Melanchthon and others told him that while there had been some violence, the extremists were now being curbed and things were under control. But shortly after his return to his refuge at Wartburg, a group of spiritual "prophets" from Zwickau reached Wittenberg. These people were men of great sanctity but little judgment. Although they excited considerable respect because of their patient sincerity, earnest piety, and remarkable knowledge of Scripture, they were very dangerous to the peace and well-being of whatever town they visited. For example, they were convinced that a new social order was dawning in which all class distinctions would be abolished, no formal education would be required (since the Holy Spirit would tell men what they needed to know), and no commerce or business activities would engage men's time. Everybody would live in simplicity under the direct guidance of the Holy Spirit.

Luther was no fool. He saw that this teaching would create an upheaval in the German homeland that would destroy most of the values of European Christian civilization. Furthermore, his own teaching had envisaged no such extreme application of the gospel. What Luther had wanted was freedom for the Christian man to live in faith. He had not advocated revolution and social disorder. Nor did he wish his own name and his teaching about justification used by those who seemed to have no sense of moderation and who were prepared to act as if people already lived in the kingdom of heaven. So, in March, 1522, against the wishes of Prince Frederick and, of course, defying the ban of the Holy Roman Empire, Luther returned to Wittenberg to stem the extremists.

His problem now was a different one from that which had engaged him a few months and years before. Then he had been fighting for the purification of the Catholic Church, the recovery of the essential gospel, and the right of God's children to live in freedom under God's love and righteousness. Now he had to fight against people who assumed that freedom and license are the same thing. His earlier battle had been for true freedom under God; the new battle was against anarchy in religion with its inevitable result in anarchy in social, economic, and political affairs.

The reform must be carried on, Luther said, but it must be carried on by preaching, teaching, writing, the simple life of faith, and responsible action, not by violence, physical upheaval, and the attempt to overthrow the whole order of things. If people lived in true faith, if they opened themselves to the gospel of God as love, if they worshipped God in the Holy Communion, if they cared for their neighbors, then all would be well. It would take time for the implications to be worked out, and people must be allowed to move as slowly as their particular grasp of the gospel demanded. Those who did not yet see the meaning of freedom in Christ were not to be coerced. In other words, orderly growth and not revolution; rejection of idolatry but not iconoclasm, or the "smashing of idols or symbols"; brotherly sympathy rather than violence and revolt —these were the methods, the ways in which true reform would occur.

In any case, Luther did not agree with the extremists that the old Church and ancient customs were bad. On the contrary, Luther had a rather conservative streak, which made him feel that much in the old Church and old customs was good. Why demolish statues if they help people to grasp the true gospel? Why refuse to wear the traditional church vestments and sing the old music if these are beneficial? The test in each and every matter was simple enough: did the practice or custom aid God's children in their response to Him and in their duty to help their fellowmen? Leave the churches as they were; continue whatever practices were useful and helpful; do not disturb established customs. Those things were not what mattered, for they were *adiaphora,* a Greek word which can be translated as "incidental" or "unessential." The important thing was God's love for men and the trust which men placed in that love.

Luther's position, which might be described as the middle way between the tyranny of ecclesiastical authority and the anarchy of sheer individualism, was regarded by the extremists as intolerable conservatism. They believed that he had deserted the cause which he himself had led. They could not grasp his point when he said that "there is much that is Christian and good under the papacy." Indeed, he said, everything that is Christian and good has come from the ancient Church. All that it needed was purification, the centering of attention on the essential truths, and the rejection of all ecclesiastical tyranny.

These remarks seemed to convey to the extremists that Luther really did not wish to carry out the reforms he had argued for. Of course, they were wrong. Luther did wish the reforms to be brought about, but he did not think that reform and revolution were the same thing. He wanted freedom and love, not the overturning of everything that existed. He saw that the extremists, who interpreted the Bible as if it were a book of laws governing society and every aspect of life, were imposing a new kind of legalism—a legalism which was in detail different but in attitude identical with the churchly legalism against which he had fought so valiantly.

Luther won the battle. Men who had been attracted by the Zwickau "enthusiasts" saw their mistake. The "prophets" were not entirely crushed, for they continued to gain a few followers, and there emerged the "anabaptist" community, a rather small and uninfluential Christian fellowship. But the great majority of Germans who had been caught up in the movement started by Luther remained loyal to his teaching or were won back to it within a short time. Now there were two ways in which people could be Christians in the German states. One was the old way of the established Church; the other was the new way which Luther had opened up.

There was as yet no formal separation, however, between the Catholics and the Lutherans. The latter thought themselves to be as much members of the Catholic Church as anybody else. They did not believe that they were any less loyal to the true Church than their fellow Germans who followed the more traditional ways. But events would not permit this situation to continue. Sooner or later, a separation was bound to take place.

In September, 1522, Luther's translation of the New Testament was published. Its success was immediate—at last the German who could read his own tongue had the source book of Christian faith available to him. Once again, Luther was back in Wittenberg, where he faced the formidable task of organizing his followers. He also had to consolidate what the reform had accomplished, now that the extremists were no longer complicating matters. He began to think of translating the Old Testament—something he would not accomplish until twelve years later. First, the Holy Communion, or mass, must be put into German, so that worshipers could really participate in it. Furthermore, some kind of constitution must be divised for the Christian fellowship if those who followed Luther were not to fall victim, once again, to anarchy and confusion.

Besides all this, Luther was regularly preaching sermons in Wittenberg and elsewhere in the neighborhood. The sermons had to be prepared carefully, so that the point of his reform was made clear. He had to continue writing tracts and pamphlets, expounding the significance of the Lutheran breakthrough. And he was especially concerned with the problem of Christian morality in the light of the principle of justification. If Christian man is free, how is he to regard the ethical teaching which for so many years had governed his daily life and social relationships?

One of Luther's sayings concerning this has often been quoted. In Latin it is *pecca fortiter,* "sin boldly." Obviously such a quotation out of context can seem an invitation to the most gross sort of evil living. But in context it does not mean that at all. What Luther really said was, "Sin boldly—since man is bound to be less than his best, seeing that he is not yet perfect—but believe all the more boldly." Or, since everything a man does is less than the perfect fulfillment of God's will, do whatever you are doing with all your might and main, not letting yourself waste time and energy worrying over whether this or that act is entirely and completely the right one. That is the way the old ethics taught you; the result was nothing but fear of doing wrong and a terrible sense of despair about ever being able to please God. But in all that you do, put your whole trust and confidence in the goodness and love of God; have faith in that love. For God cares for you; he understands your imperfections; and if you honestly try to love your neighbor, doing the best you can in any circumstance, God will accept what you do, will forgive your mistakes and wrongdoings.

That paraphrase expresses what Luther did mean. Luther himself had experienced the paralysis of will and the doubts of mind which come from fussing every minute about one's actions. He had discovered what happens when one attempts to "earn salvation" by doing "good works." To be in such a state is utterly unchristian. Luther now knew that when a man trusted God, he could be sure that whatever he did he must do *fortiter* ("heartily"), without assuming that it was absolutely, perfectly, completely right. Every man is "both a sinner who has been forgiven by God and a man who in fact does sin." This seems paradoxical. But like so many apparently contradictory statements, it expresses a deep truth. Nobody is perfect. Yet we can do our best, with all our heart and strength. Martin Luther's point is that this is what God wants of us; this is what he requires of us.

It is obvious that such a position was open to misunderstanding. The Lutherans were charged with "antinomianism"—complete disregard for all moral law. Although untrue, the charge compounded the already complicated internal condition of the German states. And there were other problems, too. When the German knights—the old nobility and aristocracy—attempted to regain the power that they were losing, they tried to use some of Luther's ideas for their own ends. Luther was forced to speak out against them. And when peasants in various parts of Germany began to revolt against their rulers, they found inspiration and support in the teaching of the extremists, with their notion that the kingdom of heaven had been established immediately on earth. Groups of peasants wandered around the countryside, plundering the rich and even killing opponents in the name of "Christian freedom." There was an enormous amount of destruction. In some parts of the German territories all social order seemed imperiled. Once again, Luther spoke out.

His criticism of both nobles and peasants rallied the mercantile class and a number of German princes, dukes, petty kings, and rulers to his side. They saw that far from being an incendiary who wished to turn everything upside down, the reformer of Wittenberg was a man who stood for social and political peace, for the maintenance of order, and the respect due to normal civil government. Unquestionably, Luther was a vehement man, and when excited, he could say things that in his own heart he did not really believe. In opposition to the wild peasant revolt, he urged the princes to arrest and, if necessary, slay the hordes who were ravaging the land. It was his vehemence and not his intelligence which was talking. At the same time, he did want the continuation of a decent, orderly social and civic power, even while advocating all measures that would secure genuine justice and do away with poverty and want among the underprivileged classes.

A few years before the peasant revolt, Pope Hadrian IV had tried to enforce the ban on Luther which had been adopted at the Diet of Worms. In 1522, another diet was held at Nuremberg and papal representatives put their case before the assembly. But Lutheran ideas had already spread over all of

Germany and had begun to influence other parts of Europe as well. The princes at Nuremberg refused to reaffirm the Edict of Worms, for they feared that civil war would break out. As a consequence, Luther's cause was given another period of relative freedom, and during that time, more and more people were won to his side. Germany became a divided land. In some places the Lutheran way was firmly established. In other places, the older way was still accepted. Separation was becoming a fact, even before it was recognized in any official sense.

In 1524, at a second diet in Nuremberg, the ruling princes once again considered the "Lutheran question." On April 18, the diet issued another edict: "The gospel should be preached in accordance with the interpretation of the universal [or Catholic] Church. [But] each prince in his own territory should enforce the Edict of Worms so far as he is able." What this really said, despite the lip service to the Edict of Worms, was that in each part of Germany, the ruling power could decide whether the old ways were to be continued or the Lutheran way adopted. At the diet held in Speyer from June 25 to August 17, 1526, it was once again decided not to enforce the Edict of Worms. Instead, each of the German princes was to be allowed to act in the matter of religion, "as he would have to answer to God and to the Holy Roman Emperor." In other words, the fact of separation was now given a theoretical and legal basis, so far as the German states were concerned.

From 1526 to April, 1529, when a second diet was held in Speyer, this theoretical and legal recognition of separation produced its practical result. Most of the northern part of Germany adopted the Lutheran way, as did the southern cities of Augsburg, Ulm, Strassburg, Nuremberg, and, of course, Wittenberg. In what is now Switzerland, the city of Constance accepted Lutheranism, and a few years later Basel became "reformed."

Maximilian, the brother of Charles V, presided at the second diet in the absence of the emperor. Charles had finally seen the futility of efforts to suppress the Evangelicals, but Maximilian tried to take a harder line. His adamant determination to apply what might be called "the mailed fist" brought about the unity of all the reformist groups in Germany. They must stand together now against every effort to put down the movement.

The Edict of Worms was reaffirmed at this second diet in Speyer, but it was made to apply only to those parts of the empire which were specifically Catholic territories. It would have been impossible to enforce it anywhere else. A general council of the whole Catholic Church would be called to give full attention to the situation. Until then, those who followed Luther's way should more or less be tolerated. The diet demanded full religious liberty for all old Catholics in the areas where the Lutherans were in control, but it did not allow the same freedom for Lutherans in the Catholic territories. This proposal naturally outraged the reformist leaders, and they made a vehement protest against it.

This "protestation" by the reformers gave them a new name. Now they were called "Protestant," the word which still describes non-Roman Catholic Christians. It is a word that is much misunderstood. The Latin word *protestare* does not mean to take a negative position; it does not suggest denial. Its proper meaning, in the Latin which the reformers used at Speyer, is "to bear witness." What the reform men at Speyer were doing when they made their protest was bearing witness to the gospel as Luther had helped them to understand it. They were also expressing their rejection of the Speyer demand that they should grant full tolerance to Catholics but that Catholics need not be entirely tolerant of them. In their own phrases, "they must testify publicly before God that they could consent to nothing contrary to God's Word." For them "God's Word" meant God's self-disclosure through Jesus Christ as loving and good, accepting men as they were and helping them to be His children. To bear witness to that Word was the reformers' whole concern, and they vigorously claimed the right to make that witness everywhere.

Luther was not alone as a leader of the continental

Reformation. John Calvin in Geneva, Ulrich Zwingli in Switzerland, Martin Bucer, who taught at many places, Philip Melanchthon at Wittenberg, and others in Britain, where word of the movement had begun to exercise the minds of theologians, were all caught up in a general movement for the reformation of the Church. In England, King Henry VIII had written a vigorous criticism of Luther. For this the papacy gave him the title that each English sovereign still holds. It may be seen on British coins: *Defensor Fidei*, "Defender of the Faith." Yet even in England, the Reformation was bound to take place, as it did in Scotland, where a vigorous movement of reform was to get underway.

All the reformers were not in complete agreement with each other, but the Reformation had gone too far and had won too many adherents in Germany and elsewhere for the official Church to put a stop to it. The best that could be done was to recognize the facts.

On June 25, 1530, a great number of reformers from most parts of central Europe met in the city of Augsburg. Melanchthon had prepared a Confession of Faith, in which he tried to state clearly the position of those who had worked so long for the reform of the Church. Melanchthon was a great scholar, influenced by the Renaissance spirit, and a man of moderate and quiet temperament. This was not a violent document, but essentially a straightforward,

103

balanced, and generally acceptable statement. Luther was pleased with it, and he believed that the very moderation of its phrasing would commend it widely. When first presented, the Confession spoke only on behalf of Lutherans in Saxony, where Luther and Melanchthon lived. It was revised, but not drastically, and in its complete form was generally accepted (although the Swiss reformers refused to accept the section dealing with the Holy Communion, and prepared a statement of their own). But granted the few dissenting voices, the Confession of Augsburg was adopted as a definitive expression of the faith held by all those who followed Dr. Martin Luther of Wittenberg. The Augsburg Confession became, as it still is, the confession which unites Lutherans, or Evangelicals, throughout the world.

The Confession is a long and highly theological document. It begins by affirming that it is a statement of the Catholic faith—meaning the "universal" Christian belief ("catholic" is Greek for "universal"). It asserts the Lutheran doctrine of justification by faith, but it does not go to extremes in denying all freedom of the human will nor in rejecting the good works that men can do. Concerning most major Christian doctrines, it is not at all radical, and most of it could have been accepted even by Catholics. However, on the meaning of the Eucharist, or Lord's Supper, it is plainly Lutheran. The Augsburg Confession takes the form of a commentary on the

Apostles' and Nicene creeds, two ancient brief professions of faith used in the worship of both Catholic and reforming churches.

The separation between the old Church and the reform was now an established fact and a recognized reality, and so it has continued for centuries. Only in our own time, as men have come to see more deeply what Luther was driving at when he spoke of the gospel and justification, is that separation losing its importance.

CHAPTER VII

Luther and the Other Reformers

Although Martin Luther had spearheaded the reform and all other reformers were deeply indebted to him, they did not all agree with him in every respect. A good deal of Luther's time, from the mid-years of the 1520's, was spent in correspondence, controversy, and conference with other reformers.

The authorities had refused tolerance to Lutherans anywhere in Germany, but it was almost impossible to enforce that decree. Although it was not always easy to be a Lutheran in the Catholic territories, by and large, the reformers were left alone. And the years of relative freedom in the German states, as well as elsewhere, gave the reformers time for study and thought. Perhaps if there had not been such freedom, the differences among the reformers would not have become so sharp. A common defense might have kept them from differing on so many issues. However, differences did arise, and sometimes they were sharp and acrimonious.

For instance, the trouble between Luther and the extremists led by Carlstadt had ended, but the controversy was by no means over. The Anabaptist group continued to exercise some influence in reform circles. Luther had been much troubled, during the earlier period, by the lawlessness of this group. Increasingly, however, it was their theological position that worried him. The term "Anabaptist" means "above or beyond baptism," and the extremists, or spirituals, taught just that. They claimed that baptism by water, which almost all Christians practice, was not important in Christian life. What was necessary was a special gift of God's Holy Spirit, which would so inspire a believer that he need not bother with the usual ordinances and customs of the Christian community. He could trust himself to the Spirit; that was enough.

Of course, one immediate consequence of this view was that the spirituals had no use for the regular church services and felt no need to support the institution. They were prepared, if necessary, to destroy all church buildings. They were also contemptuous of education, even though Carlstadt and other leaders were learned men with advanced academic degrees.

Luther believed that such an attitude was dangerous to orderly living. He was also convinced that the spirituals' basic mistake was that they tried to be *more* spiritual than God himself. If the Bible was taken as the standard for Christian belief and life, it showed that God had immersed Himself in the things of this world. He had come "in the flesh" in Jesus Christ. He had willed that men should recognize His presence through simple earthly things, such as the bread and wine which people eat and drink to keep themselves alive. To use the traditional religious language, it was through "sacramental means" that God wanted men to find Him, although they would never find Him if they did not have absolute faith and trust in Him. In other words, men do not get to God by running away from the ordinary realities of life.

Luther was certain that it was both ridiculous and biblically untrue to think that an ideal human society, in which everybody would share equally in everything, could be realized on earth. Men must work hard for justice, but this world would never become identical with the kingdom of heaven. No

109

civil justice is required in heaven, for each man loves every other man perfectly. Luther was a realist in these matters.

For these reasons, and for other specifically theological ones, Luther was sure that the spirituals were greatly in error. And the way they acted brought great harm to the reform cause. It made people think that Christian freedom meant sheer license and that "liberty in Christ" was equivalent with anarchy in society.

Another difference among the reformers was in the attitude taken toward the outward forms and ceremonies of religion. Some of the Swiss reform leaders, especially Zwingli, seemed to think that the worship of God "in spirit and in truth" must take place in a bare room, without ornaments or music. They said that these forms and ceremonies were not explicitly prescribed in the Bible, and, therefore, not justified. Christians, they argued, must use nothing which the Bible does not direct them to use. And where in the Scriptures is the order to have musical settings for prayers, or the directive to decorate a church building with stained glass? Where are the words concerning statues of Jesus or the great saints?

Luther had an answer for these men. He maintained that all the outward forms and ceremonies were not essential but were helpful for many, and perhaps most, people. If the ceremonies were not exalted to a place of absolute importance, there was no harm in using them. That is why Luther did not want churches emptied of the statues which had graced them; why he wished to keep the rich decorations which were so familiar to Christians; and why he desired, and helped to write, hymns and chorales that would be so filled with "the holiness of beauty" that ordinary men and women would be brought to realize "the beauty of holiness." Luther was something of an artist himself, and he believed that art could be an instrument of faith. His opponents could only reply that bareness and utter simplicity were what the Bible demanded. Luther answered that the Scriptures did not forbid forms and ceremonies. All they prohibited was the substitution of forms and ceremonies for God himself, which would be idolatry.

Another disagreement concerned whether or not anything could be known about God apart from Jesus Christ. John Calvin, as much a Christ-centered man as Luther, spoke out on this issue, and in later years the theologians who followed Calvin developed his point. Later it was denounced by some of Luther's successors as *extra Calvinisticum*. This meant that in the Calvinist variety of reformed Christianity, Jesus Christ was indeed central and unique, yet elsewhere in the world God had been at work preparing for the coming of Jesus. In the language of the theologians, the "Word of God" is specially and uniquely in Jesus, but God also has other "words" for his children.

For Luther and his successors this position seemed to imperil the central affirmation of Christian faith. It is likely that Luther was wrong on this issue, but he did have an important point to make. It was Jesus, and Jesus only, who had given Luther the ability to trust in the goodness and love of God. Any position, theoretical or practical, which imperiled that trust must be looked upon with great suspicion.

Between the Lutheran and Calvinist ways of looking at the Christian faith, there is a difference in the emphasis put upon faith itself. For Calvin, the motto was *gratia sola*, by God's grace alone. For Luther it was *fide sola*, by *faith* in God and by that alone. This disagreement was about words and not about facts. Both Luther and Calvin were sure that God came first. It was God's loving concern for men, which their theology called His "grace," that was the moving power in the world. Both of them were sure that such grace could only be accepted when an attitude of utter trust, or faith, was awakened in men. Indeed, when Luther was speaking very carefully, he always spoke of "grace accepted by faith," and his doctrine of justification included the words "by grace through faith alone."

There was one other relatively unimportant difference among the reforming groups. It con-

cerned the relationship between the religious dimen-
sion of life and the civil, or political, side. Luther
was prepared to give considerable room to the political side. He was entirely opposed to any Church in-
terference in the affairs of the State, except when the
State tried to deny religious liberty. On the other
hand, in Zurich, where Zwingli was the chief reformer, and in Geneva, where Calvin eventually had
that position, the situation was much more of a
"theocracy." That is, Church and State were two
sides of the same coin. The Church could, and
should, control the affairs of the civic community.
After all, these reformers said, God was the ruler of
all of life, not just what went on in the church building or in men's souls. In their belief, it was necessary
that the divine rule be expressed in every area of
the civic community. When the Puritans settled in
New England, this was their view, too.

All these differences concerned relatively minor
issues, but the reforming groups also had two major
disagreements. The first centered around the meaning of the Holy Communion, and the three chief opponents were Zwingli, Calvin, and Luther. As we
know, the Swiss reformers felt obliged to dissent
from that portion of the Augsburg Confession which
dealt with this subject. At a conference held at Marburg in 1529, just before the Augsburg meeting,
Zwingli and Calvinist theologians, as well as Luther,
Melanchthon, and others, met to unite all reform-

113

ers. But the conference had the opposite effect: it pointed up the profound disagreement among them.

At that time practically all Christians believed that when bread and wine are set apart for Holy Communion, as Jesus commanded in the New Testament, after solemn prayers Christ himself is present in these earthly things. Traditionally this service, which dates to the very earliest days of the Christian fellowship and which Saint Paul, during the first century, described as the only specifically Christian act of worship, is a remembrance of Jesus' own death on the cross. It has also been understood as a way in which Christians thank God for all He has done through Jesus—therefore, the common name *Eucharist,* which is Greek for "thanksgiving." Christians feel themselves knit together in a strong brotherhood by common participation in this service. And above all, they sense a genuine presence of Christ with them. But how is this presence to be interpreted?

There have always been differences of opinion about this. Some Christians have stressed the sense of Jesus' actual presence; others have emphasized that in remembering Jesus' death on the cross, they participate in his "sacrifice for the sins of the world." In Catholic Christianity, the Holy Communion is regarded as being in itself a sacrificial action. Christian believers are identified with the Lord they worship and are enabled to receive the "benefits" (the help and favor) which He has bestowed on men.

Luther had already had some controversy about the Lord's Supper, or Holy Communion, with the Anabaptists. Carlstadt had contended that the service is a devotional reminder, for the believer, of the suffering and death of Christ. Luther had rejected this view, for it seemed to make the whole act far too human and it seemed to deny that it was God in Christ who was the chief agent in the Communion. Zwingli believed that the Communion is the appointed way in which Christians commemorate their Lord, thankfully remembering Him and all He had done for them. For Zwingli, it was "a confessional recital," an action in which words were said and things were done to express Christian belief and to thank God for the historical event of Jesus. The bread and wine were only bread and wine, even after they had been set apart for the purpose of the Communion. There was no genuine presence of Christ in the service, excepting an awareness of Him in the mind of the believing Christian who was present. Actually, Zwingli believed more than this, but this was the way in which Luther understood him, both before and after the Marburg Conference. And Luther was obliged also to reject what he understood to be Zwingli's position.

The associates of John Calvin held a different interpretation. They would not agree to any actual presence of Christ in the bread and wine of the Communion, but they were sure that by eating the

115

bread and drinking the wine the believer was "raised to the heavenly places," and there became a partaker of the very life of the Lord. Jesus himself, after his resurrection, was in heaven. He did not "come down" again to earth in the bread and wine. Instead, by the work of the Holy Spirit, the believer "ascended" to be with Christ in heaven. Those who received the Communion also received Christ's dynamic, or powerful, presence in their hearts and souls. The difference between Calvin, Zwingli, and the Anabaptists was in Calvin's emphasis on God as the chief actor in the service, rather than the other two groups' emphasis on man, man's mind, man's thought or feeling.

Martin Luther insisted that the Lord's Supper was much more than a commemoration. It was God's grace, or loving will, seen in action. It was a proclamation of the gospel, in that it brought Jesus into the world and into the lives of his followers—not just into their minds, but into their whole beings. Luther once said that what was announced in preaching was actually received in the sacrament—God's forgiveness, God's loving presence, the union of the believer with God in Christ through complete faith and trust. It was God's act. Man was at the receiving end, but man did not originate it.

Although a number of minor differences were resolved at Marburg, no agreement could be reached on Holy Communion. And so another dramatic moment took place in Luther's life.

As the discussion went on and on, Luther insisted on accepting the simple and direct meaning of the biblical words about the Communion and rejecting any views which might overthrow that meaning. He scratched on the conference table some Latin words which he kept covered. Then, at a crucial moment in the discussion with the Zwinglians, he revealed the words. They were *hoc est corpus meum*, "This is my body." These are the words which, according to the New Testament gospels, Jesus said as he took bread, blessed it, and gave it to his disciples. Luther said that he would not move from those words. Upon them he took his stand. Attempts to suggest that the words might be interpreted in different ways did not affect him in the least. For Luther at Marburg, as at Worms, the gospel itself was at stake. The words were Jesus' own, and they must be taken exactly as they stood.

Zwingli was in tears when he realized that no agreement was possible. He pleaded for the peace of the Church, for unity among all reformers, and urged that he wanted nothing so much as to be accepted as a brother Christian, despite the disagreement. But there was nothing to be done. The conference ended on friendly terms, with a willingness to tolerate different positions, but Luther still maintained that the gospel demanded that the scriptural words—there on the table—were to be taken as they stood. Luther did not have any special theory to explain why this must be so. Although theologians devised such theories, Luther simply insisted on the words themselves. He admitted that *how* these words could be true remained, like most matters of faith, in the realm of mystery.

The second major difference among the reformers concerned the question of "how free is free will?" This disagreement involved Luther and Desiderius Erasmus, one of the great Christian writers and teachers of the day. Erasmus was a Dutchman, a very learned scholar, and a follower of the "humanism" which was characteristic of the earlier Renaissance movement in Italy and elsewhere. He never left the Catholic Church, yet he was sympathetic with much in the Reformation movement and his influence was strong. It is not known why Erasmus did not join with the reformers. Some say he was too timid to identify himself with a movement that might have endangered his life. Others think he was convinced that reform could best be effected within the old established community.

Luther had great respect, as did the whole learned world, for the scholarly ability of this man. On the other hand, he thought that Erasmus was inadequate as an expositor of the meaning of Scripture and he felt that the Dutchman's theology placed too much confidence in the reason of man. Luther believed that human reason was incompetent to bring men to God.

When Erasmus published a book entitled *The Freedom of the Will,* Luther read it with great interest. He was shocked and even infuriated. Erasmus had dared to say that man can make choices which will help him toward pleasing God. He had argued that to deny man's will is to turn him into a slave, to refuse him the right of free decision, and to reduce him from his God-given status of genuine responsibility as a free man. Talk such as this, Luther declared, "seized him by the throat." It seemed to strike at the very heart of the Christian gospel. As Luther understood that gospel, it asserted beyond any doubt whatsoever that man is helpless before God, and his reason and his will are impotent. In civic, political, and social affairs, Luther thought that men did have a certain genuine freedom.

Certainly, Erasmus had common sense on his side. But Luther knew from his own experience that all his efforts to please God, through discipline and prayer and fasting and good works, had been entirely unable to bring to him the peace, security, and assurance that he wanted and needed. Only simple faith in the love of God and Jesus Christ had done that for him. Once again, Luther was prepared to stand or fall by the conviction born of this experience.

Erasmus received a reply to his book in Luther's

publication entitled *The Bondage of the Will*. It was obvious that the two men could not be reconciled. They approached the issue from different standpoints. Luther was concerned with the question of man's eternal salvation; Erasmus with the question of man's moral responsibility to do the best that was available for him. Luther accused Erasmus of levity and impiety. Erasmus said that Luther was arrogant and likely to drive men to terrible desperation by his teaching. Luther answered that this was exactly what he wanted to do. Only when men are desperate enough to acknowledge their absolute helplessness before God, their inability to do what is pleasing to Him, and the sense of utter loss which follows, will they throw themselves, in sheer faith, into the arms of love which are always waiting to receive them. Erasmus, Luther said, was altogether too reasonable, too confident about man and man's capacities. But the facts, he said, showed Erasmus to be wrong.

Erasmus replied to Luther and accused him of having an "arrogant, insolent, rebellious nature." He concluded with the rather devastating words—in view of Luther's naturally irrascible temperament and well-intended but stubborn spirit—"I should wish you a better disposition were you not so marvellously satisfied with the one you have. . . ."

And that was the end of the matter. It seems a shame that they could not be reconciled. If Erasmus could have been persuaded to come out frankly and openly on the side of the reform movement, his influence might have been enormous. But he died a Catholic Christian, although a critical and dissatisfied one.

Despite the differences, Luther did not spend all his time arguing with his fellow reformers. Most of his efforts were constructive and positive. When he was forced into controversies, he was personally convinced of the positions he took, and he was prepared to argue for them. He may have seemed "arrogant" and "insolent," as Erasmus charged, but his spirit was that of a man who has undergone so tremendous an experience that he simply must present his case and stand for his convictions. Luther was a man with a cause. And any man with a cause is likely to be vigorous, even vehement, in its defense.

CHAPTER VIII

Luther's Life at Home

When seen apart from the religious controversy he caused, Martin Luther is revealed as a warm, loving, generous, humorous, and attractive man. He was what the Germans call *gemütlich*, a sympathetic and kindly person, and what an older English idiom describes as "a homebody."

Although Luther had said, "Will the people at Wittenberg give wives to monks? Well, they won't give one to me," he was wrong. In June, 1525, years after being released from his monastic vows, he was betrothed to Katherine von Bora. There was certainly no reason why he should not have married, since he himself had made it clear that neither Scripture nor sound theology forbade a priest to take a wife. He had probably not done so before because he was constantly in peril of his life, denounced by both the Church and the civil authority of the Holy Roman Empire. When finally he did decide to marry, he made the arrangements very quietly, and even his closest friends were surprised when they learned that, in an almost entirely private ceremony, he had been betrothed to Katherine. A few days later, on June 27, the actual marriage took place in the parish church of Wittenberg, with a religious rite, followed by a dinner and a dance.

Katherine von Bora was one of a group of nuns who had "escaped" from a convent two years earlier and had come to Wittenberg. She had been influenced by Luther's preaching, and when she and her nine companions found themselves without any means of support she had appealed to him for help. He had already taken over the Augustinian cloister at Wittenberg and he gave the women shelter there. Soon some of the former nuns married, while others took work in the town. When Katherine married Luther, she was twenty-four and he was forty-two.

Just why Luther decided to marry Katherine is not really known. Once he remarked that he was interested in marrying one of the other nuns. In any event, it does not seem to have been a love match at the beginning. Luther said that he "esteemed" his wife but had not been "infatuated" with her. Perhaps, he married in order to please his father, who was still living.

As years passed, however, Luther and Katherine did come to love one another very deeply, if letters are any indication. In that time, marriages were very often arranged. Sometimes one's family found the right partner; sometimes the marriage was a matter of social convenience; often it was an agreement between a man and woman who liked each other but were not really passionately devoted. Modern Western ideas of courtship and marriage are not entirely new, of course, but neither have they always been accepted. In many cultures they are not accepted now. Yet once a marriage had been arranged, a couple often found that they grew to care very much for each other. Living together establishes a relationship in which genuine affection can, and frequently does, grow. That was certainly the case with Luther and his wife.

From drawings and other representations, it seems that while Katherine was not a particularly beautiful woman, she was pleasant to look at. And she was not only devoted to, but very good for, her brilliant husband. For one thing, she cleaned the house in which he lived. His years as a monk had not helped Luther learn how to keep house. Once, he admitted, he had not even bothered to have his bed linen changed for months! But Katherine was a good housekeeper, and kept the home spotlessly clean. She saw to it that Luther's needs were provided for. She made him eat regularly, and she looked after him when—as so often—he was ill.

The house which they occupied was the old Augustinian cloister which Luther had taken over when it had been closed down. There were some forty rooms in the vast barn of a place. It was not only their residence, but also a kind of headquarters for the Reformation. Visitors came in a continuing stream to consult Luther about problems of one sort or another. Conferences and planning sessions for Reformation activities were held there. Luther gave lectures in a large room of the old cloister. People who had been driven from one part of Germany or another, due to their sympathy for the reform, found refuge in the house. The job of supervising all these activities must have been enormous, but Katherine Luther took it in good spirits. She was cheerful and friendly, doing the housework and managing the servants without bothering her husband.

Luther's marriage was good for him. If it did not achieve what Melanchthon had hoped—curing Luther of a certain emotional instability—it did give him the security and happiness of his own home. Furthermore, with the birth of their children, it brought out a family devotion in him. He and

Katherine had six children, and Luther was utterly devoted to them. It was especially in his relationship with them that the very winning and lovely side of his personality showed itself.

The first child, Hans, was born on June 7, 1526, and Luther showed him all a father's love for his firstborn son. He wrote some extraordinarily tender letters in which he sent his love to the little boy. The other children were Elizabeth, Magdalena (Luther was particularly devoted to her, too, and her death at fourteen was a dreadful blow to him, for she had become his favorite child), Martin, Paul (who later became a medical doctor), and Margaretha.

In the earlier years of their marriage, Luther had financial worries. Katherine did not bring a dowry. Her mother had died when she was young, and her father, who later had bundled her off to a convent, had remarried. He never gave her any money. As for Luther, no monk had any savings, of course, and after his release from his vows, the only money he received was from friends and supporters or from fees for his teaching. All he really owned, at first, were his books. As the years went on, the Prince Elector helped him considerably, doubling his salary at the university and for church duties, and giving him outright the cloister which was now his home. Other friends and supporters provided extra funds from time to time. But Luther was an appallingly bad manager. His careless generosity to those in need was at times embarrassing, since his papers promising payment to such persons sometimes could not be honored—there was just no money to do so.

One of the regular features of life in the Luther home was the gathering of the student boarders who lived in some of the small rooms which had formerly been monastic cells. These young men ate their meals at the family table, and they treated each occasion as a chance to get their revered master to talk more freely than was possible in lecture and sermon. They wrote down what he said and are responsible for *Table Talk*, the collection of notes taken by students and friends as they listened to Dr. Luther day after day. The "talk" is, of course, disconnected and directed to particular topics in no special sequence. For those who admire Luther as a man, even when they do not always agree with his ideas, this collection is very valuable. It is composed of pithy, vivid, sometimes beautiful, occasionally almost vulgar, material. Luther sounds just like what he was: a man of the people. He did not much like the idea of "being taken down," but he did not want to disappoint his students, so he permitted them to quote him. Katherine disliked the business, but she knew it was good for her husband to relax and talk freely.

As examples of the *Table Talk*, Luther said: "Printing is God's latest and best work to secure the spreading of the true religion in the world." "Birds do not have faith. They fly away when I come into the orchard, although I intend no ill for them. In just the same way we men lack faith in God." "They are trying to make me into a fixed star. As a matter of fact, I'm a wandering planet." "What lies are told about relics! Somebody claims to have a feather from the wing of the angel Gabriel; and the Bishop of Mainz says he has a flame from Moses' burning bush. And tell me how it happens that eighteen apostles are buried here in Germany when we know that Christ had only twelve of them?" "A dog is the most faithful of animals and would be much more highly esteemed if less common." One day when there was a heavy rainstorm, Luther said, "Praise God for it. He is giving us a hundred thousand gulden worth. It's now raining corn, wheat, barley, wine, cabbage, onions, grass, and milk. We get all the goods we have for nothing. And then God sends us his only Son. What do we do? We crucify him!"

Katherine knew that it was bad for Luther to drink too much wine, so she persuaded him to drink beer instead. However, the charge that he drank too much is false. Like most Germans of the time, he was fond of beer. It promoted good feeling and friendliness. So far as is known, Luther was never drunk. But he did like to eat, and to eat well.

There was a garden attached to the old cloister, and Luther made it his own province. He grew lettuce, cabbage, peas, beans, melons, and cucumbers.

The Luthers also had a small orchard outside Wittenberg, where they raised grapes, pears, apples, peaches, and nuts. There was a fish pond filled with trout, carp, perch, and pike. Later, as his financial situation became a little more secure, Luther purchased a small farm which he gave to his "dear Katie." She spent a few weeks there each year, managing it and seeing that beef, pork, and other meats were available for the feeding of the enormous Luther household.

As a man of his own time, Luther had some definite ideas on marriage and the Christian family relationship. He believed that marriage was a right and natural state of life, providing both the companionship and the physical satisfaction which are required if men and women are to live a good life. But his view of marriage was also patriarchal. He thought that the husband should be the head of the household and that the wife should honor and obey him. There was to be love between the two, but the husband was the ruler. However, he must rule "in gentleness" and not by force. Children were to obey their parents, for this was the order of things that God had established. Such obedience was part of faithfulness to God, who had set up families so that the human race would be propagated and so that people would find security in the small unit composed of father, mother, and children.

Luther has been quoted as saying that the wife

has only three areas of competence: managing the children, looking after the kitchen, and going to church. However, Luther did not originate the saying; it is a typical German adage. He did say that wives are especially suited by physique and temperament to care for children and to run a house, and it was taken for granted that they (and men, too, for that matter) should be devout in performing their religious duties. Marriage was essentially designed to perpetuate the family through the birth of children, and to maintain the social order.

Luther's view of marriage was much closer to the traditional sacramental one than to twentieth-century ideas. The modern concept of marriage has been influenced by the "romantic" ideas first associated with the courts in France and by the humanism which was a result of the Renaissance. Although Luther was in many ways a humanist, he never applied it to his picture of marriage and family. He believed that the best marriages were those in which the couple was not so infatuated with one another at the beginning that they failed to see the necessary material requirements of that union. They would grow into love, but it was not essential that deeply passionate feelings should be there at the start. In this respect, of course, Luther's own experience as a married man verified his position.

But he also came to think that the married state was a "school for character." Dr. Roland Bainton has pointed out that, for Luther, marriage took the place which the older monasteries had once occupied. It was "the training ground of virtue and the surest way to heaven." Husband and wife learned how to live morally by the very fact of their living together. Children were a help, since it required both patience and firmness to train them. And the children themselves learned to become good and honorable people through their life with parents, brothers, and sisters.

One of the ways in which people acquire character, Luther thought, was through the very differences and disagreements which exist between them. This was particularly true in marriage. So it is not surprising that Luther and Katherine had their occasional quarrels. One of the troubles was that their daily programs did not coincide. Luther had his teaching, writing, and the other responsibilities which were inevitable for a leader. Katherine had her household duties. When she was tired of these and wanted to be with her husband, he was busy. When he was exhausted from his work and wished to have his "dear Katie" close by, it was not always possible. Naturally, such a situation led to misunderstandings. But they did not endure for very long.

It is moving to read Luther's tributes to his wife. She was not only his spouse but also his dearest and closest friend. Once he said that while in the first days of marriage, a couple experience what he called "a drunken love," when they have lived together for a long time "real marriage love" comes into the picture, and that includes the "union of mind and manners." He told Katie that she had "a husband who loved her" and this was better than being "an empress." When she was very ill, he cried out, "Katie, don't die and leave me." And when he himself was ill, so ill that he believed he was soon to die, he said to his wife, "My very very dear Katie, if it is God's will you must accept it. You are mine and you can rest assured of that. . . . God's will be done and may He always care for you and for Hans." Katie replied that she was certain of the truth of what he said and that she was sure that "God will take care of us all."

Luther's affection for his wife was equaled by his love for his children. This is shown in a delightful letter which he wrote to Hans, when the boy was four years old.

"My dearest son," Luther began, "I am glad to know that you learn well and pray hard. Keep on with it, my boy, and when I come home I shall bring you a whole fair. I know a lovely garden where many children in golden frocks gather rosy-red apples under the trees, as well as pears and cherries and plums. They sing and skip and are very gay. They have fine ponies with golden bridles and silver saddles. I asked the gardener who these children were and he replied, 'They are the children who like to pray and to learn and to be good.' And I said to him, 'My dear man, I too have a son, and his name is Hans Luther. Could he not come, too, here into this garden and eat those rosy apples and pears, and ride a fine pony, and play with those children?' And the man said, 'If he likes to pray and to learn and to be good, he too may certainly come into the garden, along with Lippus and Jost [two of Hans's young friends] and when they all come here together, they shall have golden whistles and drums and fine silver crossbows.' But it was pretty early in the day and the children had not yet had their breakfast, so I could not wait for them to start their dancing. I said to the man, 'I will at once go and write to my dear son Hans and tell him to work hard, to pray well, and to be good, so that he may indeed come into the garden. But he has a dear Aunt Lena and he'll have to bring her too.' 'That will be quite all right,' said the man. 'Go and write to him.'

"So, my darling son, study and pray hard and tell Lippus and Jost to do this, too, and then all of you will be able to go and play in that lovely garden together. May the dear God take good care of you. Give my best greetings to your Aunt Lena and kiss her for me. Your loving father, Martin Luther."

A modern child might not understand, and perhaps would not appreciate, this letter. But no one can read it without sensing something beautiful and tender in Luther's feeling for little Hans. He understood his boy; he knew what would please the child;

he was aware of the kind of toys and other playthings which delighted him; and he wrote with deep affection. Letters like this—and there are other similar ones—show a side of Martin Luther's character which is often forgotten in his fame as a theologian, a preacher, a controversialist, and a leader of the Reformation.

When he was at home, Luther loved to play games with his children. He planned special festivities for them on holidays, and he wrote songs for them. One of his songs has often been quoted. (The translation is from Bainton's *The Martin Luther Christmas Book*:)

Our little Lord, we give thee praise
That thou hast deigned to take our ways.
Born of a maid a man to be,
And all the angels sing to thee.

The Eternal Father's Son he lay
Cradled in a crib of hay.
The everlasting God appears
In our frail flesh and blood and tears.

What the globe could not enwrap
Nestled lies in Mary's lap.
Just a baby, very wee,
Yet Lord of all the world is he.

135

Martin wrote this carol for children. It is charming in its simplicity, expressing the very heart of Luther's own discovery of the gospel. Martin Luther, the fighter for reform, had a tender, simple, and loving side. Perhaps it is this combination of profound thought, valiant courage, and deep feeling that makes Luther such an interesting historical figure.

Luther also had a great capacity for friendship, and even when he and his friends did not agree, their personal affection remained unchanged. Almost everyone who knew him seems to have liked him, despite his changes of mood and his utter frankness in expressing his opinions.

Luther's friendships from earlier days continued through the years. For instance, Luther and Dr. Johannes von Staupitz had kept in touch. Von Staupitz had never embraced the cause of the reform, but he was not without deep sympathy for his former protegé. Luther always remembered that von Staupitz had looked after him, counseled him, and delivered him time and again from despair. "He saved me from hell," Luther once said when he was speaking of the old man.

For some time just before his death, von Staupitz had not written to Luther, and the younger man became worried. Had his activity for purification of the Church somehow alienated his friend? Had he hurt the old man in some fashion? He wrote a letter to inquire, and von Staupitz replied, in part: "My love for you is unchanged, passing the love of women. . . . You seem to me to condemn many external things which do not in any way affect 'justification. . . .' My dear friend, I beseech you to remember the weak. Do not denounce points of indifference which can be held in sincerity, although in matters of faith I would not have you silent. We owe much to you, Martin. You have taken us from the pigsty to the pastures of life. If only you and I could talk for an hour and open to each other the secrets of our hearts. I hope that you will have good fruit at Wittenberg. My prayers are with you."

Soon afterward, Luther's old teacher died, but he and his counsel were not forgotten. Perhaps one of the reasons that Luther always insisted that the "good and Christian things" in the old traditions should not be abolished was his reverence for this old friend whom he had so much loved. In any case, their relationship was typical of the man, just as was his tenderness and love for his wife and his children.

CHAPTER IX

Political
and Social Ideas

L uther supported the German knights in their struggle to retain some of their old power. He probably did so because many members of the knightly order had come to his aid and protection. His violent attack on the leaders of the peasant revolt and his denunciation of the peasants themselves, when they ravaged the countryside, was due to his innate respect for social peace, the preservation of civic order, and the necessity for worldly justice.

139

But Luther also had a theoretical justification for his views on the nature of society and the importance of political life. It depended on what has been called "the doctrine of the two kingdoms." The idea is expressed in a book of Saint Augustine, the Christian thinker of the fifth century, to whom Luther was deeply indebted. In his *City of God*, Augustine writes about two "cities." Both of them are present in this world and all men must live simultaneously in both of them. One of the cities—by which Augustine meant patterns or orderings of human existence —is the City of God. This is where God's love is perfectly and completely expressed. Whenever men live by God's love, they share in that city, and the Church on earth is meant to be a foretaste of the full reality of God's heavenly city. But because this world is limited and because men have a tendency to seek their own desires, the City of God is never completely realized in this world. The other city is the City of Man. In this city, it is necessary to have social institutions, government, laws, judges and courts, even armies, so that justice may be guaranteed to all and the equilibrium of human existence in the world may be maintained. Every man's life, Augustine thought, is lived in both cities, but the important question is whether a man is setting his real desires on God's city, where there is love for all, or on the earthly man's city, where, at best, justice can be obtained.

Besides reading Saint Augustine, Luther read the Bible to discover how the affairs of men should be organized. He found in the Scriptures, so he believed, that God had ordered men to respect and reverence the state, or civil government; to obey the laws; to seek for justice and to give justice; not to be rebellious against lawfully constituted authority excepting when that authority tried to prevent one from fulfilling one's Christian duties. Both the kingdom, or city, of God and the kingdom of this world were instituted and ordained by God. The kingdom of God was concerned with making it possible for men to have peace, inner security, and the assurance of acceptance by God. That was absolutely necessary if men were not to sink into despair and rest content in an almost animal-like existence. The kingdom of man was concerned with seeing to it that everything possible was done to promote the temporal happiness and welfare of the human race. In Luther's own words: "God has himself ordained and established this secular realm and its distinctions, and by his Word [his self-revelation in the Holy Scriptures] he has both confirmed and commended that realm and its distinctions. For without them we could not endure living in this life."

Although Luther had a sense of humor, enjoyed being with other people, kept many friends, and delighted in his homelife, he tended toward a rather pessimistic view of man and the human condition.

Martin Luther

He could not share the optimism which Erasmus felt about man's capacity to do something really pleasing to God. Once again, it was Luther's own experience which brought him to such a gloomy conclusion. But if man is so radically a sinner, then the kingdom of this world, the secular society, serves still another purpose. It checks the selfishness of human beings. It prevents them from devoting themselves entirely to getting what they want, and it forces them to live together in some sort of community in which they may be of help to one another.

Therefore, the rules of the state, and the laws which had been devised, were necessary to keep men from running wild and turning the world into a jungle. The ordinary laws of nature and the regulations adopted by society acted as a restraint on men's evil impulses, therefore social customs and habits must be respected and esteemed. Obedience to the civic authority was required.

On the other hand, in the kingdom of Christ the only rule was sheer love. Here forgiveness must be accorded to other people for their faults and their wrongdoings. And here was found an openness of spirit, and a willingness to accept others and to be accepted by them. But the earthly society could not yet be organized on that principle. Earthly rulers must themselves be good, honest, and just men, and so far as was humanly possible, they must try to bring

142

a little more of the spirit of love into the society they controlled.

Luther stated this doctrine of the two kingdoms very simply: "The rule in the kingdom of Christ is the toleration of everything, forgiveness, and the recompense of evil with good. On the other hand, in the realm of the emperor, there should be no tolerance shown toward any injustice, but rather a defense against wrong and a punishment of it, and an effort to defend and maintain the right, according to what each man's office or position in life may require."

Thus, the Christian believer lived in the two realms simultaneously. And there was always tension between the two. In every important decision, one had to choose which of the two sides to stress. For example, concerning a judge who presides over a lawcourt, Luther believed that in his personal life and in his relationships with his family and neighbors, the judge (if he were a Christian believer) must be a loving, forgiving, tolerant person, never seeking vengeance, and always ready to act in the spirit of charity. Yet when the judge was on the bench, handing out justice to offenders against the law, he could not act in this fashion. He must be absolutely impartial. He must not let his charity and compassion interfere with the passing of the sentence which the established law required that he give. He might feel profound forgiveness and friendship for a thief, but he must condemn him to prison if that was the legal punishment for his offense.

The judge might feel that he is in an almost unbearable situation, but that is the price we pay for being human. That is the penalty for being part of the human race, with its proneness to wrongdoing.

Luther also had more positive, cheerful, and encouraging things to say about Christian life. No Christian should try to escape from the world, with all its problems and contradictions. The attempt to escape was the great error of monks and nuns, he thought. God had put us into the world, and in the world we must live. We should not, and we dare not, try to run away to some heavenly spot where we can forget the tensions of life. In putting us here, God had set us in relationship with other people. We must live with them and work with them. Therefore, a Christian should be, in one sense, a very worldly man. But he was worldly with a difference, for the nonbelieving man did not have the deep peace, inner security, and assurance of God's love. It was that peace, that security and assurance, that enabled the believer, said Luther, to perform all his worldly responsibilities in an ungrudging fashion. He would not complain, he would not be lazy, he would not show anger. He would not be dishonest or lustful or greedy. He would have to make sacrifices and he would be glad to make them, because he would know that in doing so he—like Jesus Christ—was helping others.

Furthermore, Luther said, even the man who does not believe in God as love, and who thinks of himself as completely atheistic, cannot help serving his fellowmen in some way. The very fact that he must live together with others makes it necessary to get along with them. In getting along, he must curb his selfishness to some extent, and work out a mode of existence in which the common life might be promoted.

No one should try to overthrow the social patterns of human existence, such as was suggested by the spirituals and by the peasants in their revolt. To do that would be to defy God himself, since it was God who had established what Luther (following Paul) called "the powers that be." Perhaps this explains the tendency in Lutheran Germany to accept too easily, and without question, the government of the day. Yet Luther was no supporter of tyranny and suppression. With all respect for civil authority and the established order of things, he was equally insistent on justice for everybody. He was prepared to rebuke rulers who were despots, and he had no patience with anyone's claim to be superior to his fellows. All men were equal and all must be treated equally—with justice and in fairness.

Finally, despite his rather pessimistic attitude

about man and human affairs, Luther never thought that the world was essentially an evil and wicked place. True, it was limited and finite, with men prone to self-assertion and wrongdoing, but it was also God's world, and He could be trusted to see that somehow, someday, it would become a genuine reflection of His kingdom of love and forgiveness.

CHAPTER X

Luther—Writer
and Theologian

Luther did have definite political and social ideas, but they were not his main concern. He was primarily a theologian, writer, and preacher.

Many people tend to think that theology is an incredibly complicated subject, but it is really quite simple. It is the attempt to make an orderly arrangement of what people know about God. Christian theology is the attempt to define God's purpose and His true nature, in terms of Jesus Christ. For Christians,

Christ is the most important event in history, since they are convinced that God is most clearly disclosed in Jesus' life. Jesus becomes a kind of window through which men can come to their best and fullest knowledge of the divine being.

A theologian does not spin theories without basis in fact. He starts from the world as it is and tries to understand what God as the creator of that world must be like. A Christian theologian starts by thinking about Jesus Christ and trying to understand what God must be like if His character is truly disclosed in what Jesus said and did, what people He did things for, and what light He throws on human experience.

Martin Luther was not only a theologian; he was above all a *Christian* theologian. His thoughts about God, about God's nature, about what God has done and will do, about the world which God has created, about men and women as God's children—all of this starts from and returns to Jesus Christ. Luther was preeminently a "Christocentric" thinker; Christ was for him the center of God, the world, and man.

Many theologians are systematic in presenting their beliefs. They follow a logical, or rational, order in writing. They talk more like a mathematician than like a poet or a novelist. But Luther was not at all like that. His theology is neither orderly nor logical. It stems from particular questions or problems which he had to face. He was not a theoretical thinker, although he did have many theories. He was a man who, on the basis of his own experience, engaged in thought in an effort to make sense of what he knew in his own life.

When Luther used the Bible, as a Christian theologian is bound to do (for the Bible tells about Jesus Christ), he was not systematic either. He most often turned to the Scriptures to answer the questions and problems which concerned him at the moment. Of course, he wrote extended "commentaries," as they are called, on many of the books in the Bible. But even then, his main interest was practical, not speculative or theoretical. His question was always: What does the Bible say to *me*, to *us*, about the problems we have to face as human beings?

Yet, even though Martin Luther did not put his theological convictions in order, modern theologians have tried to do so in an attempt to understand the reformer's deepest thoughts about God and the world and man.

1. For Luther, the basic question about God was not theoretical or speculative. It had nothing to do with "proving" that God exists or discovering some evidence that He reveals Himself in nature and history. The basic question was: How does a man stand before God? How do *I* stand before God?

Luther believed that it was not crucial for man to learn about God and His relationship to the world. What was crucial was for man to discover his

149

own personal relationship with God. The beauty of nature does not lead man to believe in God, and the evil in nature does not cause man to question God's existence. Luther insisted that nature's beauty revealed God only to those who already—and for other reasons—believed in Him. For those who did believe, the marvels of nature could well be a testimony to God's greatness, His creative skill, and His control of all things. To those who did not believe, nature could be a terrible and frightening series of weird occurrences, driving a man to utter dread. But of itself, nature would not bring man to God. On the contrary, Luther thought that the greatness of nature, on the one hand, and the obvious fact that nature is without moral guidance, on the other, had the effect of making many people disbelieve in God.

The same is true of human history, since all through history (as Luther saw it) the unjust and the wicked triumphed while the good people suffered. Sometimes a good man appears to win the victory, but in time he is cast down. Certainly an unrighteous nation, perhaps like the ancient Babylonians or the later Romans, does collapse, but there is no guarantee that the collapse will come in time to save the righteous and to vindicate the cause of justice in the world. God is found in history only if first we believe in Him.

Furthermore, human experience cannot bring us to God. Luther's own life had made it clear, to him at least, that much of what happened to a man seemed more like the work of a devil than of God. If we look deep into ourselves, he said, we do not find the goodness of God there. What we do find is a mass of lies, deceit, evasions, and wicked motivations. Even the people who seem to be good are not really so, and we would know it if we could penetrate into their secret existence.

Finally, philosophy can not disclose God. Luther, of course, was taught this by his teachers of the Ockhamist school. Human reason was good enough for a factual problem, and there was no excuse for failing to use reason wherever it was likely to bring results. But it was useless to answer the questions: Does God exist? How can men know Him?

So, Luther believed that nature, history, man's personal experience, and human reason were of little or no use in coming to know God. A man should not ask himself whether or not God existed, but should try to see how he, as an individual, stands before God.

2. How does God make Himself real? How does He disclose Himself to a man? Luther said that God reveals Himself in two ways.

First, God discloses Himself in what might be called a negative way. Because a man cannot find God in nature or reason, history or experience, he is thrust into despair and lives in "fear and trembling." This is a terrible world, said Luther, and unless human beings have some deep faith it is impossible for them to live in peace and happiness. God also discloses Himself in another negative way. Not only does He put men in terror by His apparent absence from the world of nature and history, but He also speaks in dreadful judgment through the conscience of each man. When men try to be good, they judge themselves to be bad. When they feel that they have done the right thing, they are still in doubt and fear that they have done right only because it "pays off" in the long run. And conscience itself can be very deceptive, for we can think about our moral duty in such a way that we fool ourselves, even if we do not fool other people.

Second, God reveals Himself to men in Jesus Christ. This was the very center of Luther's theology. Jesus Christ is the sole self-disclosure of God to men.

In Luther's quest for "a gracious God," he felt that, apart from Jesus, God appeared a terrible judge of men and a ruthless ruler of the world. God appeared in the awful facts of nature and history and as the moral judge of man's thought, words, and deeds. But there was also God's *opus proprium*, His real nature and His true self. And that true self was loving, gracious, kind, gentle, and forgiving to every man. The Christian gospel was the proclamation that this was indeed the case—God *is* like that. We can believe it because in Jesus, who is the embodiment of God, we see gentleness, goodness, kindness, and forgiveness embodied in a true man, who loved people enough to be willing to die on their behalf. In this way, God showed Himself to the world as the genuinely loving Father. It was as if He put up a great poster announcing that God is love. This poster was not a piece of heavy paper but a real, living human being named Jesus Christ.

Yet even Jesus could not bring men to God unless they accepted him. That was what faith was about —committing oneself to Jesus Christ by fully surrendering one's life to him. It was absolute trust in him. It was the willingness to put all one's confidence in him. In a sense not unlike a person who is deeply in love with another human being, a man must give himself wholly and totally to Jesus Christ. People in love often speak of "giving their lives" into the keeping of the adored one. "I am yours," they say. "Take me and care for me." In the same way, they must surrender themselves to Jesus Christ. Not only to Jesus as the best and finest man who ever lived, but to Jesus Christ as the person in whom God was disclosed.

If a man has faith in *Jesus Christ*, he also has faith in the God who sent Jesus and who was there in Jesus. And when a man has complete faith—acceptance, surrender, trust, commitment—toward Jesus, he really has found God. Or, as Luther said, God has at last come all the way through to that man. God has found *him*. Because God comes first, and He acts before man responds. Otherwise man would have nothing to respond to. God comes to man in love through Jesus. Then man says, "Yes, I answer that love. Here I am, God, take me to Yourself and dwell in me."

When this has happened, man can see that nature is not an intolerable mystery, but the creation where God is at work, not only making beautiful things but also overcoming the evil in nature. Human history is the place where God is working out his purpose, despite the wickedness of individuals and of nations. God has to fight against that wickedness, and He will overcome it. Human experience is a place where God is at work to bring men to feel their helplessness and hopelessness, and thus to find themselves driven to God as He has disclosed Himself in Jesus. Human reason, however, is still useless as a way to finding God.

3. Luther refused to speculate about how God could be explained. He declined to work out a theory which would explain just how God is present in Jesus. Luther accepted the traditional explanation, as the great Christian theologians of the past had worked it out. But this was not his real concern. He felt, as he felt about so many matters, that these things were far too high for the human mind to understand. It was better, in his opinion, to accept humbly the truth of the gospel. "To know Christ," said Melanchthon, is "to know his benefits

[the results of what he had said and done], not to understand his natures." To be a Christian, it is not necessary to have speculative information about how God is in Christ. But it is necessary to accept, in the trust which is faith, the wonderful truth that God loves and cares for us.

Man cannot work himself into faith. We often say that we "fall in love," meaning that we are moved somehow by another person, and the only way we can respond is with our own love. So faith is given to us. We do not create it by hard work, any more than we manufacture the love we feel for another person. It happens. Although this is mysterious, Luther said the mystery was to be accepted, not argued about.

4. Using the above three points as his basis, Luther developed views about the meaning of the Church, its preaching of God's word, the sacraments of baptism and Holy Communion, man's moral duty, and the destiny which God has prepared for His human children.

As a theologian, Luther wrote and published an enormous number of books. The printed collection runs to dozens of volumes which gather together everything that he put on paper.

Some of his sermons are very long, for he tended to preach freely, writing down afterward what he remembered having said. His sermon style was simple and straightforward. Unquestionably the

155

sermons were understood by ordinary people. Even when Luther preached to fellow scholars in Wittenberg and elsewhere, he did not use high-sounding phrases. He was sure that learned scholars, as well as common folk, needed to be addressed directly and in the most simple language.

Luther's collected writings also contain many of his lectures, or "dissertations." Once again, his simplicity and directness is impressive.

Also included in his writings are the so-called "catechisms," intended as the basis for teaching in church, but also providing material for parents to use when they taught their children at home. This is especially true of the *Small Catechism*, which is so simple and clear that it is still used today in many Lutheran families as a guide to instructing children in the Christian faith. The catechism does not waste time in meeting opposition, but simply affirms the Christian faith in Luther's terms. This work, along with the *Large Catechism* (intended for adults), is arranged under five headings. First, the Ten Commandments are explained and discussed so that the reader may see how often he disobeys the laws of God. Next the Apostles' Creed is described as a summary of gospel teachings about God's forgiveness to those who disobey him and His assurance of His love. After this is a section on the Lord's Prayer, in which the Christian is instructed in the way he should respond to God's love and forgiveness. Finally, there are discussions of baptism, by which Christians are established in their faith and become members of the Church, and the Holy Communion, through which they "receive in their hearts" what the gospel proclaims by word.

When the catechisms were first published, they were printed with lovely woodcuts depicting scenes from the Bible. Each woodcut was chosen to fit the particular point being made. Thousands of copies were sold, and soon every Lutheran family in which someone was able to read or write possessed one, using it for the instruction of the children or for personal study. As literacy spread, the catechisms became the prized possessions of all those who followed Luther's way. Even today, in countries where there are many modern Lutherans, the *Small Catechism* is likely to share a place of honor with the Bible in the home.

Luther also revised the Communion service, commonly called "the mass" in Roman Catholicism. He was not content with his first revision, but completed several, all in the familiar tongue of the people. The purpose of these liturgical forms ("liturgy" means public worship) was twofold: first, to rephrase the old services in such a way as to make plain the centrality of the gospel and to remove old superstitious ideas from public worship; and second, to make possible the fullest participation of the worshipers in the church services. More emphasis was given to selections from Holy Scripture, and there was also an increase in the amount of instructional material. In fact, some critics have felt that the later Lutheran service is too concerned with teaching people and not enough concerned with inviting them just to worship God. However, at that time the simple people, as well as the more learned, needed to be given instruction. Luther felt that for too long they had been merely present at services, without really grasping what was going on. In a day when the majority of churchgoers could not read, it was necessary that they learn by ear.

Luther also brought his interest in music into the church. He arranged for the revision of the chants which were used by the clergy when they sang parts of the service of public worship. Singing these parts was traditional and Luther saw no reason to abandon the practice. But he did simplify the chants, so that those who were present could understand what was being sung. He did not abandon the singing because he did not want to eliminate everything associated with the old ways, and also because church buildings had not been built for the spoken word. Sermons could be preached from a pulpit in such a position in the church that people could hear, but it was easier to sing than to say services from the church altar.

Luther was also much interested in choral music

for church services. The Lutheran chorales go back
to Martin Luther himself, and the much later Lutheran composer Johann Sebastian Bach wrote the
music for many of them. But one of Luther's chief responsibilities, he thought, was to provide hymns
which everybody could sing. In 1524, he produced a
hymnbook which included more than twenty hymns
which he had either written and composed or which
he had arranged. Many of these have become part of
the heritage of all Christians. It is perhaps surprising,
but not entirely unexpected, that "A Mighty Fortress
is Our God," written by Luther, is sung today in
Roman Catholic churches everywhere.

Of course, as we know, Luther translated the
Bible. His translation of the New Testament appeared in 1522, and the Old Testament translation
was completed in 1534. From time to time during
his life, he produced new editions with corrections
and improvements.

Luther did not translate the Old Testament by
himself. Although he had been personally responsible for the translation of the New Testament, he
wanted assistance from scholars for the Old Testament and also for revisions and corrections of the
entire Bible. For this purpose, he held a weekly
meeting with available experts in Wittenberg. He
described this gathering as his "Sanhedrin"—the
term used to describe gatherings of Jews in the pre-

Christian period. The group would meet in Luther's house before the evening meal to discuss the Hebrew or the Greek of the Scriptures, going over the material verse by verse. Then they would try to find the best German phrases for expressing the true meaning of each section. Luther was not willing to use difficult and obscure German. He himself said that he "looked into the mouth of the man on the street," observed how that man spoke, and then tried to put that kind of German into the words of the Bible.

The result was a good, if not entirely literal, translation. The German Bible was not only readable and understandable, but was also a vivid and picturesque version of the source book for Christian faith and life. Futhermore, Luther's translation was very influential upon later developments of the German language. It played a significant role in creating a kind of language which was in accordance with common usage and also capable of literary use by other writers in later years. This contribution, also made by Calvin to the French language, is only equaled by the impact of the English archbishop Thomas Cranmer on the English language. Cranmer's Prayer Book of 1549, along with the King James' translation of the Bible fifty years later, have done more than anything else—except for the plays of William Shakespeare—to shape the English language. The same is true of Luther's translation of the Holy Scriptures into German. Somebody has said that all

Germans, whether followers of the Catholic Church or of the Lutheran way, spoke Lutheran German for centuries. And Germans today, granted some modifications, still speak, write, and think in Lutheran German.

CHAPTER
XI

Luther's Last Days and His Influence

In Martin Luther's era, men aged much more rapidly than they do now. If they did not actually grow old more rapidly, they were certainly regarded as old when today they would be thought of as middle-aged. Luther died in 1545, at the age of sixty-three. But for some time before that, he had been looked upon by friends and followers as "an old man." And as an old man, he had more or less

163

retired from the active scene, although his stream of letters, sermons, and books still continued.

To some degree, his retirement was due to bad health. He still lectured at the university, gave counsel to those in need of spiritual help, and carried on his pastoral duties in Wittenberg so far as he was able. But he was afflicted by all sorts of aches and pains, and had serious trouble with his hearing. Beyond that, and much more painful for him to endure, was a series of attacks of kidney stones.

Naturally, this accumulation of physical ills affected his temperament. He had always been a man of spirit, ready to break into a fit of anger. He had been stubborn on occasion, and was liable to get angry, especially when he did not feel well. But he was not always moody. On the contrary, his long and deep friendships and the affection which his family felt for him indicate a lovable quality about him. He could complain bitterly about his ailments, speaking or writing as if he were a hypochondriac. On the other hand, he could be warm and tender. Certainly he had a keen sense of humor, a congenial manner, and a strong wish to be loving, understanding, and gentle. In other words, Luther was a normal man, granted the exaggerations which are the usual mark of a genius.

Despite his semi-retirement, Luther kept himself busy. In 1536, two years after he and the "Sanhedrin" had completed the translation of the whole Bible, he became involved in plans for an agreement—"the Concord"—with Swiss theologians. Luther had long hoped that some sort of agreement could be reached with the supporters of the old Catholic position. Finally, a sort of settlement was made, largely through the efforts of Melanchthon. Zwingli had been killed in 1531, during the second Kappel War, and Luther, with his idea that the hand of God was to be seen in all events, believed that the Swiss leader's death was a judgment of God on a minister who had become a belligerent.

There were further outbreaks by the Anabaptists —a particularly bad one in Münster in 1536. Five years earlier, Luther and others had signed a manifesto warning the Germans about the dangers in this movement. Luther felt that the discontinuance of infant baptism was especially shocking. He believed that the baptism of children incorporated them into the life of the Christian family, and provided the base from which they could proceed to an acceptance of the gospel. He used to say that when he was in a moment of despair or when his personal faith was not burning at its brightest, he always remembered, "I *am* baptized," and felt greater peace and security in his soul.

Throughout his life, and even in his latter days, faith always involved a struggle for Luther. There was so much in the world and in his own experience which seemed to contradict what he felt was the

165

truth about God's love and acceptance of him. Yet when he remembered that he was by his baptism a Christian, he could always start from there. His job, he felt, was to make real and to bring alive in his own soul what baptism in itself stood for and had started working in him.

Although Luther signed the attack on the Anabaptists he was not happy about the severe penalties, including death, which might be accorded them. To one of the statements against the Anabaptists, in which it was urged that they should be "put to the sword," he added: "I assent. Although it appears to me cruel to punish them in this way, it is even more cruel that they condemn the ministry of the Word [or gospel], have no well-based teaching, and suppress the truth, in this way seeking to turn upside down the civil order." In another addition to a second manifesto, he urged that whatever might be required in the way of severe action, in order to put down civil strife, should be tempered with the mercy which a Christian owed to his fellows.

Luther's attitude toward the Jews had become hard and stern, because he had never been able to understand why they had "rejected" Jesus. He came to feel that there was an element of evil, or sin, in this rejection. And regarding the papacy, his later years were marked by an increasing realization that no reconciliation was possible, and he attacked the Roman Catholic Church vigorously and sometimes unfeelingly. Despite the fact that he was a sick man at the time, in much pain and discomfort, his attacks on the Jews seem inexcusable. And while his attitude toward the Roman curia and its officials is at least understandable, it is regrettable that he let himself speak so harshly against those who were, of course, still prepared to persecute him and his followers.

In 1539, Luther permitted the German ruler Prince Philip of Hesse to take a second wife, although his first wife was still living. The Prince, a supporter of the Lutheran cause, had married an aristocratic lady through a family arrangement. There was no love between them, no romance, and little understanding. Therefore, Philip sought satisfaction in promiscuous relationships. But he was unhappy about his actions, and finally, he appealed to Luther. If Philip had remained an "old Catholic," some way might have been found for him to secure an annulment; then he could have married again. But this was no longer possible, since he had become a Lutheran. Luther himself was opposed to divorce on biblical grounds. What was he to advise his supporter and friend?

After much pondering and study of the Bible, Luther concluded that the Old Testament practice of having more than one wife, without (as it seemed) violating God's will, might be the solution. He said that Philip might marry again. Legally,

Luther was condoning bigamy, and shortly afterward, he regretted his counsel. He was also criticized for it. But the harm had been done. Philip did remarry, and even though his first wife agreed to the plan, it was a grave mistake. The Prince had to "buy off" the Holy Roman Emperor, by making political concessions to him, and, in the course of time, weakened the stand of the Protestants against the papacy. Although a second wife solved Philip's problem of promiscuity, it is hard to justify Luther's decision, except on the grounds that he did not understand that what the Old Testament permitted was not a legitimate practice in his time.

The "old man" also had other troubles. He was heartbroken at the death of his fourteen-year-old daughter, Magdalena. He was worried about the low standard of morality in his own city of Wittenberg, and deeply distressed by a lack of genuine piety among the citizens. He thought of leaving his home and going elsewhere, but he rejected this solution because his, and his family's, roots were now so much in that place. A few friends cheered him up, especially the great painter Lucas Cranach, with whom Luther spent a great deal of time. And he was happy in his home and with his family. He continued his writing and in 1543 published his lectures on Genesis, the first book of the Bible.

Martin Luther had been born in Eisleben. It was fitting that he should die there, too. The counts of

Mansfeld, the nearby town where Luther had gone to school, were involved in a dispute and they wanted someone to act as mediator. Melanchthon was very ill at the time. So was Luther, but he went. After he brought about a reconciliation at Mansfeld, his health broke. He was able to reach Eisleben, and he died there, on February 18, 1546.

Luther's death was a terrible shock to his friends and his followers, and a blow to his family. But his death did not put an end to the movement which he had started. Other men, not least Melanchthon himself, carried on the work. The Reformation continued even though its strongest leader was no longer alive to provide guidance. Although Luther had become the symbol throughout Europe of the reform of the Christian Church, he was not indispensable. No man is indispensable.

Luther had led a strenuous life. He had been subject to enormous risk; his life had been threatened from time to time. He had experienced spiritual distress and had been forced to struggle with the fears that never ceased to plague him. He had changed from a belief in a terrible, judging God to a belief in a God of love and mercy. It was this conviction about God which had sustained and supported him throughout his struggles, in his distress, and when it seemed that everything for which he stood was likely to be lost. The cause which was so dear to him was his very life.

Melanchthon preached Luther's funeral oration. The reformer's body was brought back to Wittenberg and the service was held in the Castle Church. People came from villages and towns in the neighborhood, and many great men of the land traveled to be there, too. Memorial services had already been held at Eisleben, but the one in Wittenberg was the most impressive. Melanchthon tried to be impersonal, but he did not succeed. He was obliged to say what he knew; and he spoke movingly of his friend's goodness, affection, and deep faith.

Luther's breakthrough, as we know, was his rediscovery of the authentic Christian gospel as found in the New Testament. This authentic gospel had often been smothered by unimportant details, by an insistence on certain ways of worship, and by a great mass of ideas, ceremonies, interpretations, and additions.

It was Luther's conviction about the gospel and justification which split the Christian world in the sixteenth century. Church officials, theologians, and ordinary people were not prepared to accept such a simple and straightforward presentation. They were too much in love with the ideas they had inherited and the practices which were dear to them.

But today the Christian world is growing closer together. Luther's discovery of the authentic gospel, along with his insistence that God accepts people because He loves them and not because they are nice people or good people or especially pious people, is seen to be the truth about Christianity. However, not everyone acknowledges indebtedness to Luther for this. Luther himself would not have wanted recognition; all he wanted was that others should reach this insight, by whatever means.

In the Catholic Church itself, one of the most important recent events was Vatican Council II, called by Pope John XXIII. At that Council, the centrality of the authentic gospel was stressed over and over again. And Pope John, like his successor Pope Paul VI, has made it clear that anybody and everybody who accepts that authentic gospel is "a Christian brother." Among Protestants, too, a vigorous movement for Christian reunification has been going on for many decades. This movement also finds the center of Christian unity in the gospel.

There are a great many problems of interpretation, and there are many different ways in which Christians worship and pray, talk and think. But in all parts of the Christian world, it is being realized that if the stress is placed on the gospel, and what it means for a man to feel himself accepted and loved by God, then less important matters will fall into place. If men put their faith in the God who is love, and who acts on our behalf through Jesus Christ, they will discover how to live together in real unity.

Martin Luther would have rejoiced in this unity, for he did not want to split the Christian family. All he really wanted was to recall every Christian to the wonderful truth of God's love and to God's acceptance of each man in spite of that man's defects. God demands of human beings only that they have complete trust in Him and live in utter charity with their fellows.

Perhaps there is no better way to sum up Martin Luther than by reading the words of his hymn, *"Ein Feste Burg."* The English translation is by Thomas Carlyle.

> A safe stronghold our God is still,
>   A trusty shield and weapon;
> He'll keep us clear from all the ill
>   That hath us now o'ertaken.
>   The ancient prince of hell
> Hath risen with purpose fell;
> Strong mail of craft and power
> He weareth in this hour;
> On earth is not his fellow.
>
> With force of arms we nothing can,
>   Full soon were we down-ridden;
> But for us fights the proper Man [Jesus Christ],
>   Whom God himself hath bidden.
>   Ask ye, who is this same?
>   Christ Jesus is his name,
>   The Lord Sabaoth's Son;

He, and no other one,
Shall conquer in the battle.

And were this world all devils o'er,
    And watching to devour us,
We lay it not to heart so sore;
    Nor can they overpower us.
        And let the prince of ill
        Look grim as e'er he will,
        He harms us not a whit;
        For why?—his doom is writ;
    A word shall quickly slay him [The "word" is the
        Gospel.]

God's word, for all their craft and force,
    One moment will not linger,
But spite of hell, shall have its course;
    'Tis written by his finger.
        And though they take our life,
        Goods, honour, children, wife,
        Yet is their profit small;
        These things shall vanish all;
    The City of God remaineth.

A Brief Bibliography

The following books, selected from a vast library which has been written on Martin Luther, may be of interest to the reader. All of the books listed are in English. No effort has been made to include any of the massive volumes dealing with technical questions of Luther's theology or the problems which have arisen concerning the controversies in which he engaged.

Bainton, Roland H. HERE I STAND. Nashville: Abingdon Press, 1959. A fine biography. THE MARTIN LUTHER CHRISTMAS BOOK. Philadelphia: Fortress Press, 1959. This is a lovely collection of carols, sermons, and other material by Luther, dealing with the Christmas season.

A Brief Bibliography

Fife, Robert. YOUNG LUTHER. 1928. An interesting account of Luther's early years.

MacKinnon. James. LUTHER AND THE REFORMATION. New York: Russell & Russell, 1962. An enormous four-volume work, primarily for the more advanced scholar, but filled with important material.

Nettl, Paul. LUTHER AND MUSIC. New York: Russell & Russell, 1948. A good study of Luther "the musician," especially for those interested in music and hymnody.

Watson, Philip S. LET GOD BE GOD. Philadelphia: Fortress Press, 1947. An interpretation of the thought of Luther by a distinguished British scholar.

INDEX

177

Index

Contrition, acts of, 69, 70
Counter-Reformation, 35
"Cradle Song," Luther, 18
Cranach, Lucas, 168
Cranmer, Thomas, 160

Devil:
  fear of, 17
  Luther's vision of, 88
  reality of, 48-50, 88
Diets. *See* Nuremberg; Speyer;
  Worms
"Doctrine of the two king-
  doms," 140-144

Eck, Johann, 6, 76, 80, 82
Edict of Worms, 84-86, 99-101
Education, medieval, 42-44
Education of Luther, 19-25
  degrees, 25, 28, 61
  higher, 25, 27, 28
  as monk, 54, 57, 61
Ein Feste Burg, Luther, 18, 159,
  172-173
Eisenach, 13, 23, 24
Eisleben, 13, 14, 168, 169
Erasmus, Desiderius, 118-121,
  142
Erfurt:
  Augustinian monastery, 52-58
  Luther a teacher at, 57, 58
  University of, 25, 27, 28, 43,
  44, 57
Eucharist, 104, 114. *See also*
  Holy Communion
Europe, medieval:
  Christianity as unifying ele-
  ment in, 33, 34
  emergence of nationalism in,
  8, 40
  political fragmentation of,
  33, 38, 39
Extra Calvinisticum, 111

Faith, 153-155
  fide sola, 112
  justification through, 63, 72,
  73, 104, 112
  reason and:
    Luther's view, 28, 119, 120
    Ockhamist view, 26, 27
    Thomist view, 26
Frederick the Wise, Elector of
  Saxony, 67-69, 78, 85, 92,
  127
  protects Luther, 79, 80, 86,
  87
Free will, 49, 104, 118-121
Freedom of the Christian Man,
  The, Luther, 81
Freedom of the Will, The, Erasmus, 119

Germany:
  Catholic-Lutheran split, 95,
  100, 101, 103, 105
  cultural unity, 40
  Lutherans, 84, 107, 108
  nationalism, 8, 40
  political fragmentation, 38,
  39
  respect for authority, 145
  universities of, 43, 44
God:
  forgiveness of, 70, 74, 75, 97,
  152, 153
  grace of, 112, 152
  love of, 65, 66, 71, 75, 97, 140,
  142, 152-155, 170-172
  Luther's relation to, 148-155
  reality and presence of, 35,
  48, 49
  revelation of, 27, 28, 151-154
  "word" of, 111, 112
  wrath of, 49, 51, 52, 66, 71,
  73, 152

Gospel, 63, 67, 84, 152, 170, 171
basic truth of, 71-73

Hadrian IV, Pope, 99
Heaven, 48, 49
Hell, 48, 49
"Here I stand" speech of
Luther, 6, 7
Heresy, Luther accused of, 79,
80, 84-85
Heretics, 32, 33
Holy Communion, 80, 96, 114,
155, 157, 158
differences of reformers on,
104, 113-118
See also Mass
Holy Roman Empire, 3, 39, 67,
83
Holy Spirit, 91, 92, 108, 116
Humanism, 118, 131
Hus, John, 76
Hymns, Luther's, 18, 159, 172,
173

Iconoclasm, 93
Idolatry, 93, 111
Indulgences, 69, 70, 73-77

Jesus Christ:
Calvinist *vs.* Lutheran views,
111, 112
embodiment of God, 71-73,
111, 147, 148, 152-155
Luther's relation to, 148, 152-
154
presence in Communion
(Mass), 55, 114-118
remoteness of, 50, 66
Jews, 32, 33
Luther's attitude toward, 166,
167
John XXIII, Pope, 171
"Justification by grace through

faith," 63, 72, 73, 96, 104,
112

Lang, Johannes, 67
Large Catechism, Luther, 156,
157
Latin language, 20
Leo X, Pope, 76
Lombard, Peter, 57, 58
Lord's Supper, 104, 115, 116.
See also Holy Communion
Luther, Hans (father), 13, 14,
16, 17, 20, 21, 28, 29, 35, 36,
41, 53, 55, 56
Luther, Hans (son) 127
letter to, 133-135
Luther, Katherine (wife), 124-
130, 132, 133
Luther, Magdalena (daughter),
127, 168
Luther, Margarete (mother),
13, 14, 16-18, 20
Luther, Martin:
alleged mental instability, 51
appearance of, 29
birth date and place, 13
character and personality of,
9-12, 29, 51, 123, 127, 136,
164
childhood of, 15-20
children of, 18, 126, 127, 133-
135
death of, 163, 168, 169
family of, 13-15
friendships of, 136, 137
interest in philosophy, 25-28,
54
love of nature, 15, 45
marriage and homelife of, 18,
123-136, 168
musical talent of, 18, 24-26
vow to become a monk, 48, 52
See Education; Monk;

Index